**If you find this book, either
enjoy it yourself or return to...**

_____

_____

_____

_____

abide

PRACTICING KINGDOM RHYTHMS IN A CONSUMER CULTURE

Published by LifeWay Press®
© 2010 Jared C. Wilson
Second Printing December 2010

ISBN: 978-1-4158-6899-7
Item: P005271630

Dewey Decimal Classification Number: 248.83
Subject Heading: CHRISTIAN LIFE \ SERMON ON THE MOUNT \ DISCIPLESHIP

Printed in the United States of America.

Leadership and Adult Publishing
LifeWay Church Resources
One LifeWay Plaza
Nashville, Tennessee 37234-0175

We believe the Bible has God for its author; salvation for its end; and truth,
without any mixture of error, for its matter and that all Scripture is totally true
and trustworthy. The 2000 statement of *The Baptist Faith and Message* is our
doctrinal guideline.

Scripture quotations marked HCSB®are taken from the Holman Christian
Standard Bible®, copyright © 1999, 2000, 2002, 2003 by Holman Bible
Publishers. Used by permission. Holman Christian Standard Bible®, Holman CSB®,
and HCSB®are trademarks of Holman Bible Publishers. Other versions include:
NIV, the Holy Bible, New International Version, copyright © 1973, 1978, 1984 by
International Bible Society.

Cover design by Micah Kandros Design.

TABLE OF CONTENTS

MEET THE AUTHOR
JARED C. WILSON

Hi, my name is Jared, and I have achieved absolute perfect "abidedness" by unfailingly walking with Jesus for more than 30 years. I am so close to Jesus, I even have special permission to make up words like "abidedness." I also make up other things, like that first sentence.

The truth is, this book about subverting the rhythms of consumerism with the counter-cultural rhythms of the kingdom of God is written by a guy with a serious Twitter compulsion who gets nervous when he leaves the house without a cell phone. So let's try this again:

My name is Jared, and I'm an imperfect disciple of a perfect King. As a follower and a leader—but mostly a follower—I have learned a few things about how the good news of Jesus impacts the way Christ-followers live wherever we are.

I grew up in the suburban South, so I know what it's like to make 5-minute fast-food runs, pay $5 for coffee, and wait behind a woman who has 20 items in the 10-items-or-less grocery checkout line. Now I live and pastor in a small rural town in Vermont where I'm more likely to hear a cow moo than a car honk. The outside pressures of consumerism are not as thick here, but I've learned that the reason suburbia is the way it is—good and bad—is because we are the way we are. I brought self-absorption and self-centeredness with me to Vermont.

Fortunately, the gospel makes all the difference.

I hope you'll find in this book not just practical helps for your spiritual disciplines, but the game-changing proclamation of the good news. That good news is that even in your setbacks and struggles, God is at work in you according to His good pleasure.

INTRODUCTION
THE KINGDOM VERSUS SUBURBIA

"I am the vine; you are the branches. The one who remains in Me and I in him produces much fruit, because you can do nothing without Me" (John 15:5).

Some parts of the Bible sound awesome until I realize I don't understand them. Once I realize I don't understand them, they don't stop being awesome, of course, but my awe is less of the "Wow!" variety and more of the slack-jawed, drooling "Ummm . . ." variety. Ephesians 5:18 is a prime example:

"And don't get drunk with wine, which leads to reckless actions, but be filled with the Spirit."

The "don't get drunk" stuff I totally understand. Tell me not to do something, and I can usually handle it. It's the other part that's confusing. How exactly do you "be filled with the Spirit"? It tells me to do something—which is great—but I have no idea how to accomplish what I'm supposed to do. How do I go about "being filled"? Doesn't the Spirit fill? How do I be something the Spirit does? It sounds as though Paul is telling me to get active about being passive.

And he is.

Though I'm still wrestling with the concept, I'm beginning to realize I'm already quite familiar with the concept of active passivity. And passive activity for that matter.

SUBURBIA

According to the 2000 U.S. Census, 79 percent of Americans live in urban or suburban areas.[1] Most people who will read this Bible study live in what we often simply call "the city" or in a suburb of the city. Every day those of us who live in these areas, particularly in the suburbs and the "nicer" areas of the city, demonstrate with our routines and attitudes that we are experts at actively being filled with the spirit of something. We're shaped by the place and the manner in which we live. By living in a certain manner and in a certain place, we give permission for this shaping to take place, though most of us aren't aware it's happening. That's the same sort of active passivity Paul appealed to in Ephesians 5:18.

If I may be blunt, the suburbs smother the Christian spirit. I know this firsthand because I've spent most of my life in suburban areas. My experience there has taught me that in most cases, both the conscious and subconscious message of the suburbs, in a nutshell, is self-empowerment. Self-enhancement. Self-fulfillment. Self is at the center, and all things serve the self (self-service!). The primary values of suburbia are convenience, abundance, and comfort. In suburbia you can have it all, and you can get it made to order in a super-sized cup with an insulated sleeve.

> WE'RE SHAPED BY THE PLACE AND THE MANNER IN WHICH WE LIVE. BY LIVING IN A CERTAIN MANNER AND IN A CERTAIN PLACE, WE GIVE PERMISSION FOR THIS SHAPING TO TAKE PLACE, THOUGH MOST OF US AREN'T AWARE IT'S HAPPENING.

Whether we realize it or not, the values of suburban culture affect us. They shape us. They slyly dictate how we think, act, and feel. And how we follow Jesus. (Or how we don't follow Jesus, for that matter.) The cultural tide of suburbia is exceedingly difficult to swim against. Almost instinctively, we feel we must have the nice house for our busy family, the nice car to get us to our rewarding job, and the nice neighborhood amenities to make all of life more livable. For followers of Jesus it's a challenge to engage in worship of Him that goes beyond a weekend church service and invades the space and time of the rest of our "real lives."

Most of us make time for God when we feel we have time, doing our best to fit Him in between the paths from house to car, car to work, work to car, and car to house. The problem is that God owns all of life, and worshiping God means we must revolve around Him, rather than the other way around. God shouldn't be confined to a compartment in our schedules. Jesus doesn't abide in His assigned time slot; we abide in Him.

But how do we do that?

RE-FORMATION

Abiding in Him is the process of formation, but that's easier said than done, since most of us have already been formed by the consumer culture we're immersed in. We've adapted quite well to the rhythms of suburbia and we've even stuck a Jesus fish on some of them. To cultivate spiritual formation, then, means to find ways to immerse ourselves in the work of the Spirit—to re-sync our lives to the rhythms of the kingdom of God.

Unfortunately these rhythms are difficult to hear and feel inside the noise of our consumer culture, which is blaringly loud even in the peace of the suburbs.

As the directive to "be filled with the Spirit" indicates, and as Jesus' command to "abide" implies, there must be intentionality and active participation on our part. But the difference between this study and other works on spiritual disciplines is a sense of relief. Many of us grew up in church environments that stressed things like quiet times, service projects, and worship services—which are all good things—in such a way as to create holy homework for the Christian life. The result, at least for me, was not kingdom rhythm but religious burden.

Often missing from my own spiritual formation attempts in the past was the central place of the good news of Jesus' complete and sufficient work. Imagine if Paul had written in Philippians 2:12, "Work out your own salvation with fear and trembling," and stopped there. It's good, solid instruction, but there's not much good news in it. A command like that is sufficient for Christian busywork, and by itself it would be successful at creating more of what it requires. But Paul didn't end the thought there. He didn't just say, "Get to work." He wrote in verse 13, "For it is God who is working in you, enabling you both to will and to act for His good purpose." Now that is good news!

SAILING

Being filled with the Spirit is like sailing. There are roughly 20 to 30 working parts on a sailboat, which means there are always plenty of tasks to accomplish when sailing.

> OFTEN MISSING FROM MY OWN SPIRITUAL FORMATION ATTEMPTS IN THE PAST WAS THE CENTRAL PLACE OF THE GOOD NEWS OF JESUS' COMPLETE AND SUFFICIENT WORK.

You will definitely break a sweat, and you have to stay attentive. But there is one thing you can't control, and it makes all the difference in the world: the wind. You can hoist the sail, but only the wind can push a sailboat through the water.

Many approaches to spiritual formation can be compared to getting into a sailboat and then blowing deep breaths into the sail. Consequently we get really tired and have almost nothing to show for our work. The approach of the study you hold in your hands, however, is to help you cultivate the conditions to best live in and enjoy the goodness of the good news. The kingdom of God is at hand. Its rhythms are at work, and they are within your grasp. As you explore these rhythms in *Abide*, I hope your affections for Jesus are renewed, and the life you've desperately needed emerges, bringing God the glory He deserves. A life that follows kingdom rhythms can be lived anywhere in the world, including the suburbs, but it requires an intentional hushing of the consumer clamor so you can focus on the heartbeat of God in the everyday things.

RHYTHM ONE
FEELING SCRIPTURE

I've hesitated to use the word "feel" to describe this vital spiritual rhythm of the kingdom, but after looking for a better word I've come up empty-handed. Don't let the word scare you, though. You don't need to look for "godly goose bumps" or another particular emotional reaction when you read the Bible. If you experience those things, that's great, but in this context "feeling Scripture" means having a deeper familiarity with the message of the Bible, a sense of its big story line, and a comfort with the diversity of its storytellers.

When I sleep some place away from home, I almost always use a night light. I'm not scared of the bogeyman, but I am afraid of injuring myself if I have to suddenly get up because one of my daughters cries or the phone rings. In a dark, unfamiliar place, just getting up to use the bathroom can become a gauntlet of toe-stubbing horrors. But when I'm at home, utter darkness is good. It helps me sleep. And when I have to get up, usually I have no problem finding my way around because I know where everything is, even if I can't see. I have an innate sense of the location of my night stand, the bathroom door, and the dresser. I can maneuver around and through these things in the dark because I'm used to doing so in the light. I never had to practice not running into things; I developed a routine from spending time in my bedroom.

That's what I mean by "feeling Scripture."

Feeling Scripture entails regular inhabitance in the Bible, learning its nooks and crannies, and developing a similar sense of familiarity that we might have with a room in our homes. Jesus liked to use the word "abide" to describe this practically instinctual sense.

But instead of developing that sense, we treat the Bible like an object of utility, not something that is life-giving and active. We read the Bible asking ourselves how we might use it rather than how it might use us.

Thankfully, as we develop our ability to find our way around it, the Bible never gets old or stale. The Bible is a book that teaches us how to read it as we read it.

MESSAGE IN A BOTTLE

A 2007 study by researchers from the Stanford University School of Medicine and the Johns Hopkins School of Public Health tested the brand and logo recognition of preschool-aged children. They discovered that, on this subject, most of these children were geniuses. Two- to six-year-olds could easily identify familiar brand names and packaging, and even if they didn't know the name of the company, they could connect the logo to the product it was most known for. Further, the researchers discovered that even if a hamburger, for instance, did not come from McDonald's, telling some kids that it did resulted in higher satisfaction with the taste than from the kids who knew they weren't eating a McDonald's burger.[2] Not only did these kids know their logos, they bought the message of the logo advertising hook, line, and sinker. Their perception actually changed their tastes.

These kids never had to study product branding. Their parents didn't quiz them with flash cards every night. They hadn't taken any classes on brand marketing. They knew their stuff because kids these days are swimming in marketing messages. Thanks to everything from billboards to book covers, television ads to television shows, radio jingles to Internet pop-ups, nobody has to study product logos to recognize them; they're part of our environment. They *are* our environment.

What are some products you can instinctively identify based on their branding?

Do you think your values have been subliminally shaped by marketing? Why or why not?

The cumulative effect of routine exposure to company branding is just one aspect of the way we're shaped by the daily messages of our consumer culture. The message is practically subliminal. None of us would assent, after all, to a letter in the mail that simply said, "Be more selfish." But that's precisely the message we're hearing—and heeding. Sure, we may laugh at the idea that buying the world a Coca-Cola will teach it to live in perfect harmony, but plenty of us live as though the

Test your familiarity with, and susceptibility to, product logos with the online Retail Alphabet Game at *joeykatzen.com*.

"For this people's heart has grown callous; their ears are hard of hearing, and they have shut their eyes; otherwise they might see with their eyes and hear with their ears, understand with their hearts and turn back—and I would cure them" (Matthew 13:15).

morning drive through Starbucks or the afternoon trip to the vending machine for a diet soda are what will keep our day on an even keel.

The truth is, the messages of the environments we're most in and the routines we most practice shape our attitudes and behaviors.

They do this in two ways: by bombarding us with their presence and by appealing to our appetites. We all know using Apple computers won't really make us cool, but the Mac vs. PC ads have succeeded like few other advertising campaigns in identifying a desirable culture—hip, witty, smart—with its product. Consequently, Apple gains more market share in the computer world every year. The company has succeeded in pummelling us with their advertising and appealing to our desire to identify with the "cool kids."

Some companies have been so successful with their marketing that their product names have actually become the common names for the products themselves. Consider how we refer to a "Kleenex" as the name for all kinds of facial tissue or say "Xerox" for making copies.

The Coca-Cola Company has succeeded in identifying their brand with America itself. Coke products and advertising are seen less as marketing and more as nostalgic vignettes of Americana. We may all laugh at what is truly implied in the slogan "Coke is it!" but Coca-Cola isn't the number-one soft drink in the world because everyone just said "Nah."

Coke was invented by pharmacist John Pemberton in 1886. Since that time, the Coca-Cola company has spread across virtually the entire planet, offering more than 400 brands in more than 200 countries or territories and delivering 1.5 billion servings each day.[3]

If we're going to maintain a vibrant pursuit of Jesus in this culture where a soda (or some other product or experience) is "it," we have to first understand how these ubiquitous messages shape our values. And then we have to learn how to subvert these messages with the more powerful message of the Bible.

Think about some of the items you've purchased in the last year, things like household products, groceries, clothing, magazine subscriptions, books, and memberships to clubs or fitness centers. What promises did they make that you had to believe in order to purchase them?

How might more exposure to the words of Scripture help you find the daily messages you receive from our consumer culture less appealing?

DOING VS. BEING

When Jesus hit the scene 2,000 years ago, He preached "the gospel of the kingdom," which people gain access to only by denying themselves. To live we have to die to ourselves. This is what "taking up your cross" means.

In this new kingdom, Jesus stood squarely at the center. But the people of first-century Palestine lived as though Herod was king and Caesar was lord. That's why in the Gospel of Matthew, Jesus proclaimed the values of this new kingdom with His version of the Magna Carta, the Declaration of Independence, and the Constitution all rolled into one. We call it the Sermon on the Mount.

The Sermon on the Mount (Matthew 5–7) is a great kingdom blueprint, a beautiful proclamation of what the kingdom of God *looks* like. It begins with the gospel of the Beatitudes, which serve as a preamble to the constitution of the kingdom. Those few verses are essentially Jesus' way of saying, "Look, this is how it's going to be now." The sermon continues to outline a glorious reality that hums and buzzes with life in the Spirit. In nearly every way, the Sermon on the Mount runs counter to the way of the world, calling us to abandon self-interest, embrace the dangerous life of discipleship, and live counter-culturally.

It's tempting for us to look at the Sermon on the Mount and read it as law rather than good news. We look at it and see things to *do*. But the Sermon on the Mount, as a picture of the kingdom, is best thought of as something to *be*. There's a huge difference in those perspectives.

When you think about the Sermon on the Mount, do you think of it as good news? Why or why not?

What's the difference between reading this list as things to do and reading it as things to be?

What we see in the Sermon on the Mount is a sweeping survey of how to live in the kingdom, complete with commands ("turn the other

R

In *The Divine Conspiracy* Dallas Willard writes that the Beatitudes "are explanations and illustrations, drawn from the immediate setting, of the present availability of the kingdom through personal relationship to Jesus."[4]

cheek," etc.). But if we read it as law, we miss the stunning truth that the kingdom is something that already exists and that Jesus is bringing. It's the difference between "making" Jesus King and recognizing that He already is. The Sermon on the Mount speaks not just to Christian behavior, but first and foremost to Christian character. And this is why Jesus reframes so many things like adultery (to lust) and murder (to anger)—so we won't see Christianity as something to do but first something to be.

> **Read Matthew 5:3-11. How are the Beatitudes like the Bill of Rights to the kingdom constitution?**

"Man does not see what the LORD sees, for man sees what is visible, but the LORD sees the heart" (1 Samuel 16:7b).

> **In Matthew 5:17, Jesus said, "Don't assume that I came to destroy the Law or the Prophets. I did not come to destroy but to fulfill." How might the knowledge that Jesus is doing the fulfilling apply to the commands we see in the rest of the Sermon on the Mount?**

> **Take some time to write out what some beatitudes of suburbia might sound like. What or who is considered blessed in a consumerist kingdom?**

Suburban beatitudes might include "Blessed are the aggressive, for they will get their own way," or "Blessed are the materialistic, for theirs is the house full of stuff."

HOOKED ON A FEELING

By now you may be wondering what Coca-Cola and the Sermon on the Mount have to do with studying the Bible. It might seem like we're taking the long way around, but being able to feel Scripture involves zooming out from the mechanics of Bible reading and study and seeing the way the relationship between the messages we hear and the posture we hear them in affects us.

Hopefully we have established two things so far:

1. We're shaped by the messages of the kingdom of the world all the time, even when we don't intend to be. And this means routine exposure has a cumulative effect of changing us.

2. The core message Jesus delivered about the kingdom of God is that the kingdom is something Jesus Himself establishes and fulfills.

When we put these two things together, the main implication for Bible study is this: If we place ourselves in routine exposure to Scripture, the message of the kingdom of God, thanks to the work of the Holy Spirit, will eventually shape us more into the image of Christ. Just as being in the world of suburbia results in a "doing" of consumerist values, "being" in the world of Scripture results in a living of the kingdom of God.

So how do we stop *doing* when it comes to studying the Bible and start *being*? The difference is in how we read it.

We tend to approach God's Word looking for an informational exchange. We come to the Bible to learn something. While the Bible contains the wisdom of God, the primary reason to read Scripture isn't to learn stuff, but to become stuff. Transformation is the primary reason the written Word of God exists. Feeling Scripture requires discipline and consistency, like most Bible study plans, but the aim of feeling Scripture is treasuring God's Word in our hearts and delighting in God's laws. We have at our fingertips the very revelation of God to us, and yet we treat Scripture like a blunt instrument, a dry reference book, or a prop for our propaganda—anything but the wellspring of God's truth.

If we're going to abide in Christ, we have to dwell in God's Word. This means meditating on Scripture, chewing on it, and savoring it. This doesn't come easily at first, but the more we do it, the more natural it feels. After a while, we will feel Scripture shaping us and we will naturally begin to live its message.

In Psalm 119:103, David wrote: "How sweet Your word is to my taste— sweeter than honey to my mouth." This is the testimony of someone who has come to thrive on God's Word, who has come to taste it and has found that it actually tastes really, really good.

I know Bible study can taste like a stale rice cake. But this isn't because the Bible isn't delicious; it's because our palette is not yet sensitive enough to discover how delicious it is. Once we acquire that taste, we

In *Follow Me* authors Greg Hawkins and Cally Parkinson reveal the findings of a major spiritual growth study conducted by Willow Creek Community Church in Illinois. They write: "Everywhere we turned the data revealed the same truth: spending time in the Bible is hands down the highest impact on personal spiritual practice."[5]

What does it mean to "abide in Christ"? Along with this resource, consider picking up a copy of Andrew Murray's classic work *Abide in Christ* to keep reading about this pivotal concept.

18   RHYTHM ONE ABIDE

can't get enough of it. It creates more demand for what it supplies. The more we dwell in Scripture, developing a greater taste and feel for it, the less sweet and less comforting the things of the world taste and feel.

"Taste and see that the Lord is good. How happy is the man who takes refuge in Him!" (Psalm 34:8).

Describe a time when reading or studying the Bible was difficult for you. What was the cause of the difficulty?

Describe a time when something in the Bible piqued your interest or captivated you and drove you to read or study more. What do you think was the difference in that experience?

What are some differences between using the Bible and drinking from the Bible like you would draw water from a well?

FINDING THE RHYTHM

The question most of us have is "How do I do this?" It can be really confusing to think about how to "be" rather than "do" without *doing* something. Learning to feel Scripture doesn't happen by osmosis. Effort is required, just as effort is required in sailing. Many times we read our Bibles as if we're in a sailboat paddling the water with our bare hands. Sure, you can do it, but it's not advisable.

There are many Bible study programs and schedules out there: memorization systems, study Bibles and devotional books, Bible reading calendars, etc. You may find some of these tools helpful, and they are, but the art of feeling Scripture isn't about a checklist or a program; it's about what happens while you're in the Word of God.

Some good options for Bible reading plans include *The NIV Classics Devotional Bible* and *The One Year Bible* (available in different translations).

A program can help you establish a reading schedule and even get you to think about what you're reading. But the practice of feeling Scripture applies to all situations in which you read and interact with the Bible. Feeling Scripture will compel you to come back to the Bible in ways a regimented program won't. This is a rhythm that, once established, won't let go of you.

Following are five ways you can get started. When put into intentional practice, these approaches can condition you to feel Scripture much more keenly.

1. Interpret Before You Apply

Because we bring the inherent message of self-centeredness to Bible study, it becomes natural to first ask about a passage of Scripture, "What does this mean to me?" Instead, we should first ask, "What does this passage mean?" This is the practice of interpreting before applying.

Let's see how this works. Jesus said that if anyone wishes to follow Him, that person must deny himself and take up his cross (Luke 9:23). When we skip interpretation, we diminish the powerful relevance of this teaching. By first asking what the Scripture means to us, we see taking up our crosses as about dealing with annoying coworkers or enduring a nagging spouse. But this application grossly misrepresents the primary meaning. Taking up one's cross is about death, not inconvenience.

This doesn't mean the passage can't apply to annoying coworkers or nagging spouses, but if we interpret Luke 9:23 to involve dying to our own desires, we're better equipped to handle situations with others in selfless ways. An annoying coworker, then, is not someone to endure, but someone to love sacrificially. Correct interpretation makes the Bible come alive—and be felt—in ways jumping to personal application simply can't.

At its root, applying before interpreting assumes that the Bible is not relevant until we make it so. But the Bible is already relevant. It doesn't need us. The Bible is what we need, but in our zeal to try and squeeze it into the confines of our particular situations, we often lose sight of its present relevance.

Interpretation before application is a fundamental element to all Bible study. It's especially necessary if our desire is to develop a greater feel for Scripture. In interpreting before applying, we subject our feelings to Scripture's unwavering revelation (interpretation) rather than subject Scripture to our feelings (what often happens in application).

How to Read the Bible For All Its Worth by Gordon Fee is a helpful book for understanding the overarching themes, timelines, and author intents of the Bible. Reading it will help broaden your understanding of what it means to get a feel for the overall story of the Bible.

In some Old Testament stories, we can run into trouble by leaping to application. Consider the story in Genesis 22 of Abraham's willingness to sacrifice Isaac, for instance.

Take another look at the Beatitudes in Matthew 5:2-11. How might applying before interpreting prohibit you from fully grasping the meaning of this passage?

Write down some other Bible verses or passages you might misconstrue if you apply before you interpret.

Listen to "Lifeblood" on the leader kit enhanced CD, an audio devotion from author Jared C. Wilson. Your group leader can send it to you via e-mail. As you listen, think about whether you're immersed in Scripture or simply using it.

2. Keep It in Context

This is one area where the effects of consumer culture are really apparent. From CliffsNotes to microwaves, we want everything we do to take as little time and require as little effort as possible. That desire extends to how we want our Bible served up to us. Even the teaching in many of our churches follows the lead of television news soundbites, giving us a verse or two at a time from different spots in the Bible. The problem is we can't see the beauty of a tapestry if we're only shown a thread at a time.

As a result of this kind of patchwork study, we over time lose a sense of the Bible's continuity and larger story. We still might hear it in little spurts, but those brief bits start to seem like advice from a fortune cookie. For instance, out of context, Jesus' statement, "I did not come to bring peace, but a sword" (Matthew 10:34), makes Him sound like Conan the Barbarian.

Out of context, Hebrews 6:4-6 seems to indicate that Christians can lose their salvation, but three verses later, the author of Hebrews contrasts whatever is being described in verses 4-6 with "better things connected to salvation" (v. 9). If we don't consider the full passage, we may lose our faith in assured salvation.

We like to keep Scripture short and manageable, and that's understandable. It's certainly more convenient that way. But we can't learn to feel it if we don't occasionally allow it to overwhelm and intimidate us. Bite-sized chunks are good for memorization and the

To help discover and appreciate the full meaning of a given passage of Scripture, consider picking up a commentary related to the book you're studying and read the historical context section as you study. Most study Bibles have an abbreviated version of this information at the beginning of each book.

like, but to feel Scripture we have to drink from it deeply and wade into its deeper waters, and we must do this continually.

What are some other verses that if taken out of context can lead to confusion or poor interpretation?

Lectio divina is a way of reading Scripture prayerfully. Latin for "divine reading," it involves reading large chunks of the Bible in an attempt to feel the emphasis of Scripture, eventually turning it into prayer and praise.

Does the idea of reading large chunks of Scripture intimidate you? What other obstacles in your life keep you from doing so?

3. Make Connections

This might be the most fun of the practices of feeling Scripture. Although the Bible contains 66 books written by about 40 authors covering all kinds of genres, the entire thing is one cohesive story, a brilliant mosaic fashioned together from the same few tiles.

One way we can get a better feel for the continuity of Scripture is to make connections between different passages. All the stories and teachings in the Bible are connected somehow; there are no coincidences. OK, that's hyperbole; there are some coincidences. Some isolated stories don't easily connect with others. For instance, it's difficult to tell how the story of Rahab helping the spies (Joshua 2) might be connected to the kid who fell asleep because Paul preached too long (Acts 20:7-11). But there are many more connections, particularly between the Old Testament and the New Testament, and between Jesus' teaching and the teaching in the New Testament letters, that testify to the premeditation of God's revelation.

There is a connection between these stories of Rahab and the sleeping child, though. Both of their plot lines involve a window.

For an example, read the story in John 6:16-21:

"When evening came, His disciples went down to the sea, got into a boat, and started across the sea to Capernaum. Darkness had already set in, but Jesus had not yet come to them. Then a high wind arose, and the sea began to churn. After they had rowed about three or four miles, they saw Jesus walking on the sea. He was coming near the boat, and they were afraid.

"But He said to them, 'It is I. Don't be afraid!' Then they were willing to take Him on board, and at once the boat was at the shore where they were heading."

What are some connections you can make from this story to another part of Scripture?

If you continue reading John 6, you will come to one of Jesus' most controversial statements. Later in that chapter, He told the crowds that they must eat His flesh and drink His blood, a statement that caused most of the people listening to walk away scratching their heads.

The most obvious connection is the parallel narrative in Matthew's Gospel (14:22-33). Thinking more deeply, however, we might be able to make other, less obvious connections, such as Jesus' declaration, "It is I," to God's revealing His name in the Old Testament, "I AM." Jesus walking on the water reminds us of the Spirit hovering over the surface of the deep in the beginning of Genesis. The boat immediately going to the shore when Jesus boarded brings to mind God separating the land from the chaotic waters in the creation story. The story itself reminds us of other stormy sea tales, like Noah and the ark, Jonah and the big fish, or even when Jesus slept below deck while the disciples fretted during a squall.

Write down any other connections you can make.

Biblegateway.com, bible.org, and lifeway.com/bible are great online resources for Bible searches and cross-references. They also include other reference tools like commentaries and word studies.

When we make connections like these, our minds are trained to read Scripture as one, continuous story, and it cultivates in us the ability to feel the breadth of Scripture. Of course this takes time to develop, but the reward is worth the time. We can't enjoy the sustenance of the Bible if we treat it like a drive-thru window.

But once we connect Point A to Point B, we have to avoid the tendency to assume they have the same meaning. Making connections simply proves that Scripture interprets Scripture, and that the more connections we make, the greater feel we have for the brilliant unity of the Bible.

As you're reading a particular passage, ask yourself, "What other passages does this remind me of?" Then track those passages down using cross-references, a concordance, or an online Bible search program. Before you know it, you'll be making connections and getting a feel for the broader and fuller contours of God's story.

4. Apply Prayerfully

When you're ready to apply Scripture—after you've interpreted it—instead of applying a passage in a static sense, do it in a prayerful, dynamic sense. Here's what I mean:

First Corinthians 13:7 tells us that love "bears all things." In a static application, we read this and may think, "This is important because my mother is really difficult to live with. She's very burdensome."

"There is no better way to pray scripturally than to pray Scripture."
— Lorne C. Sanny[6]

In a prayerful application, we read this and turn it into a prayer: "Lord, give me the strength and passion to love my mother even when I find it very difficult. Change my heart to be able to bear all things."

The first approach is basic application, and it's not necessarily invalid. But it is distressingly close to subjecting Scripture to our experience, rather than vice versa. It's also more observational than motivational. It only involves noticing something, not committing to something. That's why it's static—it lacks movement.

The prayerful approach to application, however, not only presses us to subject our feelings to Scripture—in the example above, the application entails asking God to provide strength for a difficult relationship—but it also turns the application into a conversation with the One prompting the response. Applying prayerfully takes us beyond noticing, "Hey, this reminds me of my problem," to bringing that problem before the Lord and taking the initiative to be changed by Scripture.

A static application of 1 Corinthians 13:7 can actually tempt us to gracelessness because the focus is on what must be endured (a difficult mother), rather than on the endurance itself. We can end up with an application that runs counter to the point of the verse in the first place.

In the prayerful application approach, the impetus is toward grace because the focus is on loving according to the Scripture's call in 1 Corinthians 13. Because of this, the prayerful approach to application is a highly successful way to begin feeling Scripture.

Read Psalm 119:105. How might this verse relate to prayerful application of Scripture?

Think of a pressing concern or difficulty you're facing right now. Can you think of a Bible verse or passage that speaks to your situation? Write out a prayer to God about your situation using the language of that verse or passage.

5. Look for Jesus

Luke 24 begins with the greatest moment in history, the watershed moment of great reversal: the resurrection of Jesus. This was the moment when all heaven broke loose.

But in the immediate wake of that event, the fullness of its impact had not settled on all who knew Jesus. Two of His followers were walking to a village called Emmaus when Jesus showed up. They didn't recognize Him at first, even though they'd heard news of His resurrection. In fact, they were still sad because they weren't sure if the rumors were true. Not only did Jesus affirm what they'd heard, but He also took the long walk as an opportunity to preach the best expository sermon in all of history. Luke 24:27 tells us, "Then beginning with Moses and all the Prophets, He interpreted for them the things concerning Himself in all the Scriptures."

Using the entire Bible, Jesus preached a message about Himself. And let's not forget that the "Scriptures" Jesus opened to them at that time only consisted of what we know as the Old Testament.

Referring to the Old Testament, Jesus commented in John 5:39, "You pore over the Scriptures because you think you have eternal life in them, yet they testify about Me."

From this we learn that all of Scripture either points to Jesus' life and teaching or emerges from it. All of it.

Do you have any objections to the truth that Jesus is the central character in all of Scripture? Why or why not?

How is Jesus the central character in specific parts of the Old Testament?

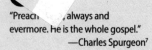
To know God, we must know Jesus. And to feel Scripture well, we must see Jesus between its lines and at the beginning and end of its many trajectories. He is there, all over the place, and Christians committed to following Him closely will seek the glorious enlightenment of the disciples on the road to Emmaus.

When you're reading the Old Testament, wherever you are, ask yourself questions like, *What does this say about Jesus? How does this point to Jesus? Did Jesus ever quote or reference this? What is the importance of this in light of Jesus?*

Finding Jesus in the Gospels is easy of course, but making the Jesus connection in the epistles is vitally important.

Scholar N. T. Wright says that we ought to read the New Testament as if Jesus is giving us sheet music for a masterwork symphony in the Gospels, and as if Paul and the other New Testament authors are playing it.[8]

If you desire to keep Christ at the center of your life, you must keep Him at the center of your Christian practice, including your Scripture reading.

Seeing how the teaching of the New Testament epistles emerges from Jesus' teaching in the Gospels is especially important today. Many scholars argue that Paul invented Christianity.

> **Take a look at Genesis 22. Where do you see Jesus in this story?**

> **Here's a harder one. Where might Jesus be in Exodus 17:1-7?**

MORE OR LESS

To strengthen our understanding of what it means to feel Scripture, let's give these exercises a practice run on perhaps the most famous story of the Old Testament. But first a warning.

Submitting to God's Word, disciplining yourself to begin benefiting from feeling Scripture, is always intentional. I have tried to set up an approach to Scripture reading that departs from an overly regimented, checklist-sort of quiet time structure that hinders my spiritual growth because it's done only out of duty. But there's no way to get a feeling for Scripture without reading it a lot and over a length of time. I'm assuming your use of this study guide is an indication that you're interested in Bible study. So since I have you here, I might as well shoot straight.

Many times, developing the ability to spend time in the Bible and to hear what it's saying is less about our aptitude for Scripture and more about all the noise that exists in our lives. We all know we could use more Bible, but we often forget we could use less of everything else. (Are you reading this session at the last minute before your Bible study group? Did you really not have time to do it earlier? Or did you just not make time?)

I've been in the church world for 34 years and in ministry for almost half of that, and I've noticed the church's gradual unfamiliarity with Scripture. We have our pet verses that serve our pet interests. We log the minister's message as our weekly Bible time. Maybe we get a bit here and there on Christian radio or blogs or on the "Christian mug" we drink our coffee out of, but the number of Christians who make a life out of drinking deeply from the written Word of God, delighting in its bountiful revelations, and finding true transformation (as opposed to mere information) in it are few and far between.

On the other hand, we quench our thirst with the surrounding culture like drinking from a fire hose. We inundate ourselves with sports and talk radio, magazines, television, movies, video games, celebrity "news," water cooler chit-chat, social networking Web sites, cheap novels, self-help books and speakers, and a myriad of other amusements and diversions. Though these things are fine in their proper doses, we suffer from mass exposure to unnecessary noise. As a result our spiritual senses are dulled; we lose the taste for Scripture.

Many times we find it difficult to plug into the Bible because our circuits are already overloaded with all the things we're currently plugged into.

If you eliminated one source of unnecessary "noise" from your life, what would it be? What would it take for you to eliminate it?

"One of the great uses of Twitter and Facebook will be to prove at the Last Day that prayerlessness was not from lack of time."
—John Piper[9]

In *The Weight of Glory*, C. S. Lewis argued that our problem as humans is not that we seek too much pleasure, but that we settle for too little: "We are half-hearted creatures, fooling about with drink and sex and ambition when infinite joy is offered us, like an ignorant child who wants to go on making mud pies in a slum because he cannot imagine what is meant by the offer of a holiday at the sea. We are far too easily pleased."[10]

FEELING THE OLD TESTAMENT'S MOST FAMOUS STORY

How about we try the Scripture-feeling exercises on perhaps the most famous story of the Old Testament? Most people know the basic storyline of David and Goliath, but you can refresh your memory in 1 Samuel 17.

Here's how this story has been applied countless times over the decades: The story of David and Goliath is about how to overcome adversity, challenges, and fears. Just like David—the youngest and meekest of his brothers—was able to conquer Goliath, all we need to do when we feel overwhelmed or outmanned is trust God, and He will help us conquer the giants in our lives.

The forms this approach takes vary. Goliath may represent something depressing from our pasts, our finances, a troubled marriage, or the challenges of a handicap or a setback. But we're always David, and the lesson is always "Be courageous and God will always help you win." Sometimes even David's five smooth stones become skills or tips to use in defeating the problem. (This is an odd interpretation to make, though, because David only used one of them.)

These applications are inspirational, motivational, and make us feel really good. The problem is that they don't give us a good feel for Scripture. They jump to a personal application before interpretation. They also make the account seem more connected to Aesop's Fables than to the rest of Scripture's storyline. And they don't feature Jesus. This lesson makes the Bible story about us, but the Bible isn't about us, at least not in its main characterization. The Bible is first and foremost about God.

Let's now use the exercises we've learned in this session to take another look at the story:

Interpreting Before Applying: We could spend a lot of time interpreting the various elements in 1 Samuel 17, from the historical and cultural backgrounds of the names and places to the spiritual significance at play between the Israelites and the Philistines throughout the Old Testament. What we see at the top level of interpretation is the basic story itself: The Philistines were powerful and ominous and the Israelites felt they were at the end of their rope. The Israelites also had a king (Saul) who wasn't exactly volunteering for hand-to-hand combat with Goliath. The basic interpretation, then, is this: An enemy threatened death, and the people of God were at a loss for how to combat it.

Goliath stood 9 feet, 9 inches tall (1 Samuel 17:4). According to the *Guinness Book of World Records*, the tallest man in recorded medical history was Robert Wadlow. Measured last in 1940, he stood 8 feet, 11 inches tall.[11]

What other elements of interpretation do you see?

Keeping It in Context: Since we're looking at an entire chapter and an entire story, we are not in too much danger of taking the passage out of context. Perhaps we're safe here.

Making Connections: Your turn:

> **What other Bible verses, stories, or symbols does this passage bring to mind?**

There was almost perpetual war between the Israelites and the Philistines. The Philistines occupied cities along the southern coast of Canaan and often made incursions against the Israelites. Many scholars believe they were not indigenous to the promised land, but came from across the sea. They were master iron workers, as revealed by Goliath's armor.

Applying Prayerfully: First Samuel 17:37 would make a great prayer:

"The Lord who rescued me from the paw of the lion and the paw of the bear will rescue me from the hand of this Philistine."

We could "own" this statement by praying, "Lord, You have delivered me in Jesus from the paw of sin and the paw of death, so I know You are my Rescuer."

Looking for Jesus: Now it's going to get really fun. The big mistake we nearly always make is placing ourselves in the role of David and some personal problem in the role of Goliath. But you're not David. I'm not David either. And Goliath isn't some problem, issue, or anxiety. We're in the story, though. You can see us here:

"When Saul and all Israel heard these words from the Philistine, they lost their courage and were terrified" (1 Samuel 17:11).

David learned his fighting skills during his shepherding days. He successfully defended his flock against wild animals, which no doubt prepared him to be a warrior later in life.

See us? We're the ones in the background, shaking in our boots.

But we don't stay that way for long. David (not us) had been anointed to represent the children of God in battle. He killed Goliath, and then for good measure he chopped off the dude's head. It's a pretty awesome story, honestly. Then we show up again:

"When the Philistines saw that their hero was dead, they ran. The men of Israel and Judah rallied, shouting their battle cry, and chased the Philistines to the entrance of the valley and to the gates of Ekron. Philistine bodies were strewn all along the Shaaraim road to Gath and Ekron. When the Israelites returned from the pursuit of the Philistines, they plundered their camps" (1 Samuel 17:51-53).

Suddenly we're not scared anymore. We're chasing and plundering, all because we have a champion. We didn't do the work; someone else did.

David is Jesus. Goliath is the sin and death that separates us from God. And we are the scared Israelites.

That in a nutshell is the story of the Christian life. The work isn't ours—it belongs to Jesus. Jesus did the work we were unwilling—and unable— to do. He killed sin and murdered death. He chopped its head off!

You have now seen Jesus in the story of David and Goliath, which means the story is no longer something read out of obligation, but good news that transforms your life. Think of how different it might feel to read Scripture not as stuff to "do" but as stuff to "be."

There's no doubt the Bible tells us lots of things to do. But if our Bible study feels like obligation, it won't affect us as deeply as the enjoyment of seeing the finished work of Jesus. And while it seems counterintuitive, the gospel truth is that the more we enjoy Christ's finished work, the more empowered we will be to do good works in His name.

What are some other Old Testament stories you can think of that are usually told with the Christian in the starring role? How do their meanings become more true with Christ at the center?

What is the spiritual benefit of a Scripture reading that tells us the work has been done by Jesus?

))

Tim Keller, pastor of Redeemer Presbyterian Church in New York City, is a master at discovering Christ throughout Scripture. You can read and listen to more than 150 of his sermons for free at *sermons2.redeemer.com*.

R

If you're having trouble believing that Jesus is the central character in Scripture, pick up a copy of *Knowing Jesus Through the Old Testament* by Christopher Wright. It will encourage you on your search for Jesus even in unlikely places.

THE POINT IS JESUS

Colossians 1:17 tells us:

"He is before all things, and by Him all things hold together."

The point of the Christian life is not self-improvement or more Bible knowledge, but Christlikeness. In practicing the rhythms of the kingdom, we worship Jesus and declare Him to be the King of kings and the Lord of lords. That truth should, at the very least, be reflected in the way we read the Bible. If Jesus Christ is before all things and holds all things together, there's no question that He's in a lot of the Scripture passages we read regularly. We just don't take the time to see Him.

The message we receive from consumer culture is that we are the point. We are the center of the universe, and all things revolve around us. When we buy into that, it becomes very easy to think of our time, our finances, and even our spiritual lives as belonging to us.

But all things, including us, belong to God. This truth will prove revolutionary in our lives if we declare it with our words and actions. We can begin to subvert the selfish spirit of suburbia first by weaning ourselves off the taste for its messages by cultivating a taste for the sweetness of Scripture. The good news is that this is something the Spirit does in us as we expose ourselves to the Bible's words more and more. He will not allow the Word we meditate on to return void.

Before He began His public ministry and unfurled the great kingdom blueprint for the Sermon on the Mount, Jesus went into the desert to be tempted by Satan. This temptation consisted of the same things that lure us every day: pride, power, and appetite. At one point Jesus rebuked Satan by saying that we do not live on bread alone but on every word that comes out of God's mouth (Matthew 4:4).

We can't live without food. If we want to stop doing and start being, we must begin to see God's Word as we do food—imperative for survival. That's how we can feel Scripture and abide in Christ. The Bible itself makes the connection between God's Word and Jesus (in John 1:1), and Jesus Himself makes the connection between food and Himself (in John 6:54).

Anyone else hungry? If so, then dig in. There's a place for you at the table.

At your meeting time this week, watch the video "Boats" found on the leader kit DVD. As you do, think about your own approach to the spiritual disciplines. Does it line up with any of the examples?

A CLOSING PRAYER

"Speak, Lord, for Thy servant heareth. I am Thy servant. Give me understanding that I may know thine ordinances. Incline my heart to thine ordinances . . . Let Thy speech distil as the dew.

"The children of Israel once said to Moses: 'Speak thou to us and we will hear thee: let not the Lord speak to us, lest we die.'

"Not so, Lord, not so do I pray. Rather with Samuel the prophet I entreat humbly and earnestly: 'Speak, Lord for Thy servant heareth.' Do not let Moses or any of the prophets speak to me; but You speak, O Lord God, Who inspired and enlightened all the prophets; for You alone, without them, can instruct me perfectly, whereas they, without You, can do nothing. They, indeed, utter fine words, but they cannot impart the spirit. They do indeed speak beautifully, but if You remain silent they cannot inflame the heart. They deliver the message; You lay bare the sense. They place before us mysteries, but You unlock their meaning. They proclaim commandments; You help us to keep them. They point out the way; You give strength for the journey. They work only outwardly; You instruct and enlighten our hearts. They water on the outside; You give the increase.

"They cry out words; You give understanding to the hearer."

—Taken from *Imitation of Christ*[12]

GET RHYTHM

To integrate a sense of rhythm in your life, spend a little time this week after work in a local music store. Pick up a few instruments and experiment with them. Use the space on the following pages to journal about your experience.

RHYTHM PRACTICE

View some dramatic recitations of Scripture on the Internet such as Hebrews 9–10 performed by Pastor Ryan Ferguson from the 2006 Worship God Conference. You can find this video on YouTube by searching "Ryan Ferguson Hebrews 9 and 10." Use the space on the following pages to journal about what you hear and see.

RHYTHM TWO
INTENTIONAL PRAYER

Once on a visit to Nashville, Tennessee, I found myself on one of those conveyor belt walkway things at the airport—which always reminds me of "The Jetsons"—stuck behind a guy who was just along for the ride. I wanted to walk. He wanted to hog the walkway, oblivious to the world around him, and noodle on his Blackberry. I was aggravated. I couldn't pass him up, and he couldn't see me behind him because his nose was in a gadget. Someone else might have simply said, "Excuse me," but being the introvert I am, I chose to stew in my irritation.

I grumbled to myself: *Who does this guy think he is? What a jerk! He's taking up the whole walkway. Does he think he owns it? How selfish can he be? He's so oblivious. What a self-absorbed moron!*

Then it hit me. And by "it" I really mean He, the Holy Spirit, in a lightning-quick heart smack-down of conviction. "You're being a self-absorbed moron," the Spirit said. I wasn't on a deadline. I wasn't transporting an organ for transplant. I was just doing what I always do—hurrying. For no good reason. The whole time I was aggravated with the guy in front of me for acting like the world revolved around him, I was acting like the world revolved around me, as if that guy should have subconsciously known that I wanted to get somewhere quickly and adjust his pace accordingly.

It's bizarre what hurry can do to us. I can blame my busy tendencies partly on my nervous, neurotic personality, but something else is at fault, too. The pace of life in industrialized America whispers insistently to all of us every day, "Hurry up!"

Because of my natural tendencies and the abnormally hectic pace of daily life, I find it increasingly difficult to be still. Advertisements tell me to "Act now!" Facebook and Twitter keep me up to date by the second of what everyone else is doing or thinking. Fast food restaurants encourage me to cook, procure, and eat food quickly. My inbox and calendar always remind me of my obligations and assignments. Television news bombards me with boxes and banners and tickers, a continuous feed of several ever-morphing headlines all at once. I'm drowning in noise and it all makes me anxious. Chances are, it has the same effect on you.

PRAYER AND HURRY SICKNESS

One little verse in the Bible cuts through the clutter, noise, stress, dutiful obligations, mismanaged priorities, and busyness and offers me an antidote to what ails me:

"Yet He often withdrew to deserted places and prayed" (Luke 5:16).

Does it surprise you that Jesus withdrew to pray so often? Why or why not?

What is your general attitude toward prayer? What do you wish it was?

"The sole cause of man's unhappiness is that he does not know how to stay quietly in his room."
—Blaise Pascal[13]

As I type these words right now my legs are bouncing. Why? Because I find it incredibly difficult to be still. I'm sick. I'm a jumpy person and suburbia is no help. The manicured lawns, tranquil streets, and calm of the cul-de-sacs are all lies; the peace is an illusion. Inside our homes we're buzzing with television, MP3 players, computers, cell phones, and combinations of all the above. Stress levels from homework and housework are at an all-time high. Even the drive to work, in cushioned, climate-controlled, and radio-equipped vehicles is stressful. We don't call it the "rat race" and the "daily grind" for nothing.

Even when Americans stop working, they're still working. About a quarter of all vacationers say they check voice and e-mail while on vacation. Many others refuse to take vacation days at all for fear of the pile-up of work they would face on their return. Though full-time American workers average 14 days off a year, they leave 4 unused.[14]

Once upon a time in our not-so-distant past, experts predicted that with the rapidly increasing advances in technology, Americans would have a shorter workweek and so much time on their hands for recreation they wouldn't know how to fill it. I guess we figured out what to do with all that extra time—we've filled it up with more work and more busyness. The microwave doesn't create free time; it frees up time to fill with other things, and that's just what we've done. We may think watching television or surfing the Web or playing video games is all leisure time, but the constant connection to artificial noise—visual, aural, or both—gradually quenches our spirit. And the constant filling of idle hands with idol pleasures will result in our looking like the gelatinous masses passing for humans at the end of *Wall-E*—if not physically then at least spiritually.

Pastor and writer John Ortberg writes, "We suffer from what has come to be known as 'hurry sickness.' One of the great illusions of our day is that hurrying will buy us more time."[15] In *The Life You've Always Wanted*, Ortberg goes on to define clutter, superficiality, multitasking, and speeding up daily activities as causes of hurry sickness. He warns that one of the symptoms of hurry sickness is the diminished ability to love those to whom we've made the deepest promises. Hurry sickness makes us too tired and too distracted to love well.

We immediately think of our family and friends, worrying about what our hurry sickness may cost us in our relationships with them. But do we slow down enough to also think about what it may be costing us in our relationship with God?

Are you too busy living to enjoy abiding in Christ?

God is calling us to rest in Him regularly. But we can't hear His still, small voice (or even His booming, declarative voice) because the volume on our routines is too high. We are too busy listening to the gods of the world. Further, we usually don't think to speak to Him in much more than soundbite prayers. We *can't* think to do so, because we don't make the time to think of much more than soundbites to say.

Hurry sickness causes us to be so awash in the noise of busyness that we compensate for it by accepting silence with God and loved ones.

How serious a problem is hurry sickness in your life?

What is the biggest difficulty for you in slowing down?

Do you want to reduce or eliminate hurry sickness? How do you think you could do so?

Psalm 46:10 issues the command "Be still, and know that I am God" (NIV). In Psalm 46 nations are at war, and the psalm indicates that conflicts and cultural distress prevent us from beholding God. The HCSB translates verse 10 as "Stop your fighting—and know that I am God." The NASB says "cease striving." These translations reveal what really prevents us from abiding in Christ—fighting and striving.

"Tomorrow I plan to work, work, from early until late. In fact I have so much to do that I shall spend the first three hours in prayer."
—Martin Luther[16]

MULTITASKING PRAYER VS. INTENTIONAL PRAYER

To make up for neglecting prayer, I've incorporated prayer into my daily routine. Sounds great, right? And it can be. Surely if we are to pray without ceasing, we should be praying while eating, reading, driving, paying the bills, watching movies, listening to music, reading blogs, exercising, and working at our jobs. We should bathe those activities in prayer, in part to keep ourselves tuned godward throughout our routines and in part to better "take every thought captive" (2 Corinthians 10:5) that enters our minds during times of preoccupation or distraction.

But something significant happened to me when I attempted this sort of prayer practice apart from the practice of solitary, focused prayer. My prayers became somewhat mindless. My attention was divided. I did my best to keep my internal monologue directed toward God, but too often the result felt like taking God along for the ride on my plan for the day. Prayer became just another thing to fit in. I wasn't feasting on God's presence; I was giving Him crumbs. I was multitasking prayer.

A 2009 Stanford University study published in the journal of *Proceedings of the National Academy of Sciences* revealed that concurrent uses of technology overload our mental capacity.[17] The results suggested that multitasking actually inhibits the very characteristic we think it enables: efficiency. It turns out that doing several things and consuming several things all at once not only stresses the brain, but it also prevents us from doing tasks and understanding information with accuracy.

The spiritually ambitious among us may think adding prayer to our repertoire of multiple tasks helps us better engage spiritually, but when the only time we pray is while doing other things, we program ourselves toward spiritual distortion and relational imbalance with God.

> **What is the biggest difficulty you have in making time to be alone in prayer with God?**

In Colossians 4:2, Paul commanded:

"Devote yourselves to prayer; stay alert in it with thanksgiving."

Researchers in the Stanford study concluded, "This issue seems especially pertinent in light of evidence that human cognition is ill-suited both for attending to multiple input streams and for simultaneously performing multiple tasks." In other words, our brains aren't made to receive several messages or think about several things at once.

There are two aspects to Colossians 4:2 that are crucial to proper rhythm of prayer: being devoted to it and staying alert in it.

Being *devoted* to prayer speaks to commitment, routine practice, endurance, and even duty. Being *alert* in prayer speaks to focus, clarity, and awareness.

You can be neither devoted to prayer nor alert in it if you don't commit to a time and place in which you do nothing but pray. This practice is called intentional prayer. Followers of Jesus need to commit to times of intentional solitude, with all artificial noises blocked out and adequate time to focus on talking to God scheduled in. As busy as we think we are, none of us have as large a burden placed on us as Jesus did. And even though Jesus was perfectly sinless, He still needed to disconnect, detach, and devote solitary time to the Father.

"The point of solitude is not what I do—it is what I don't do. I get away from all the voices and demands of my life and find out about what my little life is like when all the distractions are removed."
—John Ortberg[18]

Here is that verse again, cutting through the clutter of haphazard multitasking prayer: "Yet He often withdrew to deserted places and prayed" (Luke 5:16). None of us is better than Jesus. So if Jesus' practice of intentional prayer involved withdrawal to deserted places, and He did this often, how arrogant are we to think we don't have to follow suit?

The root of the English word *pray* means "to beg" and the root for the Hebrew word for pray means "to judge oneself." Both of these meanings—dependence on God and honest introspection about ourselves—intersect in intentional prayer.

Nobody can say with any integrity that they don't have time to pray intentionally. Nobody can honestly say they can't afford to do this. In fact, we can't afford *not* to do it. Jesus apparently engaged in intentional prayer "very early in the morning, while it was still dark" (Mark 1:35). But maybe for you the best time is during a lunch break or in the evening. Let's not be legalistic about times or timeframes, but let's be devoted to prayer—staying alert and giving thanks.

Jesus commanded this in Matthew 6:6:

"But when you pray, go into your private room, shut your door, and pray to your Father who is in secret. And your Father who sees in secret will reward you."

We see lots of descriptions and depictions of prayer in the Bible. We see prayers made publicly and privately, prayers of thanksgiving and petition, prayers of hope and despair, prayers of confession and exultation, prayers of celebration and mourning. Regardless of the circumstance and subject matter of the prayer, the words and actions of Jesus reveal that intentional, attentive, and solitary prayer is vital for a life submitted to the Father's will.

Where and when would work best for you to engage in intentional prayer?

What benefit do you think intentional prayer would be to your walk with Christ that nothing else could accomplish?

Many who give intentional prayer a try find extended periods of silence unnerving at first. Why do you think this happens?

"And for himself each one must speak to God and pray. You must do it for yourself, for nobody else can do it for you."
—J. C. Ryle[19]

Prayer: Finding Our Way Through Duty to Delight by J. I. Packer and Carolyn Nystrom is a guide that embraces the responsibility of praying and yet leads the reader to find joy in God's command.

RETHINKING THE DUTY OF PRAYER

I think one of the primary reasons Christians don't make quality time for prayer is because they've been trained to think of prayer in the legalistic terms of duty. I remember as a teenager dreading Sunday School every week because I knew I would be asked two questions: "Did you evangelize someone this week?" and "Did you have your quiet time every day?"

Evangelism and devotional times are not only important, they're vital for the Christian life. But having these things framed (by well-meaning leaders) in the context of duty hasn't served to make us crave time alone with God or witness to our friends. Instead we've done our duty halfheartedly, not out of love for God and neighbor but for fear of having to turn in a bad report on Sunday. Over time, the religious expectation of quiet times doesn't compel us to seek them out but instead causes us to bristle under their burden. Even 15 minutes, a blip on the radar of our day, seems too long and unwieldy for prayer, because we approach it as pure duty rather than pure desire.

Nevertheless, it's true that prayer is our duty as Christians. There's just no getting around it. In Ephesians 6:18, Paul told the church to "pray at all times in the Spirit, and stay alert in this, with all perseverance and intercession for all the saints."

In 1 Thessalonians 5:17, he was even more direct:

"Pray constantly."

> **If prayer is both vital and commanded, why do you think so few of us make time to do it?**

> **How would you describe an ideal prayer life?**

> **What do you think it means to "pray constantly"?**

Before the time of Christ, the Jews developed a number of short blessings to be said on certain occasions. Many of them, in modern language, begin with "Blessed is He . . ." and continue to thank God for the little blessings of life. Paul may have had these short blessings of the Lord in mind when he wrote, "Pray constantly."

There is no wiggle room in these commands to shirk our responsibility to pray. It's a crystal clear command of God in Scripture. Clearly, though, regimented expectations haven't worked to compel many of us to pray. However, rethinking what prayer is and what it's for does compel us. If prayer is just another thing for the checklist, it's easily abandoned because nobody grades us on it, nobody gives us a performance review based on it, and it doesn't provide the immediate satisfaction of entertainment or other leisure. In essence, we chuck prayer because the results of prayerlessness are not immediately felt or seen.

"One of the most basic things that the gospel does is change prayer from mere petition to fellowship and the praise of his glory."
—Tim Keller[20]

But if prayer is more than just another thing for the checklist, if it's instead the thing that makes the rest of the checklist doable, and if we looked not for "results" in prayer but relationship, we might find it more appealing. To put it bluntly: If there is a God of the universe (and there is), and this God of the universe loved you and wanted to be in relationship with you (and He does), wouldn't it be ignorant *not* to talk to Him? To put it more nicely, if the God of the universe is in control of our days and loves us enough to provide comfort and power for those who seek Him, shouldn't prayer be the most important part of our day?

One of the reasons Psalm 46:10 says to stop fighting and know that the Lord is God is because when we're occupied with our daily struggles, we're notoriously forgetful. As we juggle our obligations, complete tasks, run through our schedules, and consume, consume, consume, we begin to think *we* are God. We become the center of our own universe. And when that happens, prayer to the real God who covers us and cares for us seems superfluous. What's the point of telling God about the things you've already got covered, right?

Though none of us explicitly say this, both our actions and attitudes reveal this is indeed what we believe about prayer. The duty of prayer becomes heavy and burdensome because at some level, we see God as an absentee landlord or a pleasant grandfather or a last resort. But if we were to capture a sense of His greatness and wonder, of His all-encompassing might and love, of His fatherly goodness and jealous zeal, of His eternity-spanning efforts to redeem us from sin and death through the gift of Himself in the sacrifice and resurrection of His Son— wouldn't that make a difference in how we approach prayer? Or, rather, *shouldn't* it?

Where we once saw prayer as a religious act designed to merit God's favor (or the approval of other Christians), we now see prayer as an act of worship, done not to push God's buttons like He's some cosmic vending machine, but out of response to His initiative in our relationship. This is why the rhythm of feeling Scripture comes first in this study. The expectation is that as we begin to wade into God's revelation of Himself, we'll begin to experience the compulsion to reveal ourselves to Him in prayer.

Worship is always our response to God's initiative. We do not seek Him of our own initiative; He seeks us (Romans 10:20). He speaks to us, declaring salvation over us in the atoning and reconciling work of Jesus, and worship is our response to the instigation of salvation.

What leads us to think of prayer only in terms of religious duty?

How is the experience of prayer different when you see it as a response to God's revelation of Himself?

"He is as fire inflaming the soul, and making it to mount upward in prayer to God."
—Walter Marshall[21]

If God already knows everything about you, what's the value of revealing yourself to Him in prayer?

Listen to "Help!," an audio devotion from author Jared C. Wilson. Your group leader can send it to you via e-mail. As you listen, consider the level of honesty in your own prayer life.

Lazarus wasn't wandering around his tomb like a zombie until Jesus said, "Over here, dude!" No, Lazarus was dead. Jesus commanded him to resurrect and rise. In the same way, Jesus calls us forth into life, and prayer is the means by which we find our way in the newness of that life. I'm sure Lazarus, newly risen, had to wipe the haze from his eyes and find his way out of the darkness of the tomb. Maybe he stubbed his toes a few times on the way out.

Sometimes prayer can feel like that—stumbling around in the dark and walking into walls. That's OK, because we're alive thanks to the resurrection of Jesus. When someone saves your life, it's your duty to thank that person over and over again. But that duty is entirely different from the duty you feel to go to work or school every day. It's a duty of delight.

When we think of worshipful prayer as a duty, we can easily lose our taste for it. But when we think of duty as worshipful prayer, the tables get turned on the entire concept of obligation. Prayer in its essence is simply that: daily explicit worship of the One who loves us more than anyone else does and saved us in a way no one else could. Most of us have seen the difference it makes in a church service when the congregation appears as though they're there out of duty or when they look like they're there out of worship. The difference is typically the level of awareness of how amazing grace is and how good God has been. In the same way, intentional prayer is the daily private worship service of those who are awake to the amazing greatness of the gospel.

"The battle is with our own proud, self-centered inner person. Fight that battle by faith, through the gospel, in prayer. Be stunned and broken and built up and made glad and humble because you are chosen, holy, loved."
—John Piper[22]

Reflect on a time of worship that was especially meaningful to you, a time either on your own or in a worship service when you felt particularly close to God. What factors or experiences made that moment seem more special than others?

How does real awareness of God's love for us and Jesus' work for us impact our prayers?

How might you cultivate this awareness in a consistent way that makes you more inclined to the "good duty" of intentional prayer?

While addressing God as "Father" (*Abba*, in the Greek) was not necessarily unique to Jesus, it was virtually unheard of before His time. Jesus' familiarity and intimacy with God marked by His repeated use of the word "Father" marked a radical shift in how worshipers of God related to Him.

THE BLUEPRINT FOR KINGDOM PRAYER

In that big constitution of the kingdom—the Sermon on the Mount—Jesus gave us an example of what prayer in the kingdom of God should look like. We call this example The Lord's Prayer.

In Matthew 6:9-13 we read:

"Therefore, you should pray like this:
Our Father in heaven,
Your name be honored as holy.
Your kingdom come.
Your will be done
on earth as it is in heaven.
Give us today our daily bread.
And forgive us our debts,
as we also have forgiven our debtors.
And do not bring us into temptation,
but deliver us from the evil one.
For Yours is the kingdom and the power
and the glory forever. Amen."

Of course, this prayer doesn't preclude any of the other examples of prayers or commands to pray found elsewhere in Scripture, but this particular snapshot communicates to us the non-negotiable content for kingdom prayer. If we prayed according to the kingdom of suburban culture, for instance, we'd be concerned about our reputation and recognition, not God's. Our daily lives communicate where our hope and trust is placed; we are actually "praying" with our words and deeds every day. Many of our prayers may look like this:

"My self on earth,
Awesome is my name.
My success come and my will be done.
Give me lots of things I want (but think I need).
Don't even think about debt (unless it's someone else's).
Don't worry about giving in to temptation, because I deserve it.
Deliver me from guilt anyway.
For this life is mine, and the world revolves around me. Amen."

OK, so that's pretty silly. But don't we live like that, or at least fight the temptation to live like that, all the time?

Instead, Jesus' prayer is one that acknowledges our dependence and weakness but largely takes us out of the equation. It's a prayer of emptied ambition and full hope, which makes sense knowing it's a kingdom prayer and that the way into the kingdom is denying the self and embracing the crucifixion. The Lord's Prayer, then, takes the oars out of the water and raises the sail in anticipation of the sure wind of the gospel of the kingdom. Even its opening line casts our gaze above the dizzying fog of the world and toward the kingdom of heaven.

The Lord's Prayer enlarges our vision beyond the overwhelming yet miniscule offerings of our noisy, idolatrous world and shrinks our self-sufficiency to the point of basic need. Kingdom prayer is prayer that is preoccupied with God's glory.

That's how you find the rhythm of God's kingdom in a consumer culture: seeking the humility that comes from rejection of independence and admission of dependence, and embracing the confidence that comes from God's acceptance of you through Christ.

List the requests made of God in the Lord's Prayer. What do these requests reveal about Jesus' focus in prayer?

What aspect of kingdom work do you need help "bringing"?

Charles Spurgeon, in commenting on the Lord's Prayer, said: "I think there is room for very great doubt, whether our Saviour intended the prayer, of which our text forms a part, to be used in the manner in which it is commonly employed among professing Christians."

Spurgeon went on to comment that the prayer wasn't to be repeated, but to be used as a model for the way we structure prayers.[23] Find more of Spurgeon's sermons at *spurgeon.org*.

"'Father' is the Christian name for God."
—J. I. Packer[24]

"The highest goal is not that we be made holy; the highest goal is rather that God's name be hallowed. This removes man from the center of the picture, and gives that place to God alone."
—D. A. Carson[25]

"So that it is faith, faith, faith is the matter. It is no prayer that is without faith, it is but a lip-labouring and mockery, without faith; it is but a little babbling."
—Hugh Latimer[26]

What basic need do you have right now that you want God to supply?

What sin do you need to confess?

Who do you need to forgive?

What temptation do you need deliverance from?

Now turn your answers above into a prayer to the Father.

PERSISTENT PRAYER

In Luke 18:1-8, Jesus told His disciples a parable that illustrates the need for devotion to and alertness in prayer.

"There was a judge in one town who didn't fear God or respect man. And a widow in that town kept coming to him, saying, 'Give me justice against my adversary.'

"For a while he was unwilling, but later he said to himself, 'Even though I don't fear God or respect man, yet because this widow keeps pestering me, I will give her justice, so she doesn't wear me out by her persistent coming.'

"Then the Lord said, 'Listen to what the unjust judge says. Will not God grant justice to His elect who cry out to Him day and night? Will He delay to help them? I tell you that He will swiftly grant them justice. Nevertheless, when the Son of Man comes, will He find that faith on earth?'"

The character in the parable compared to God is the judge. Does this parable mean that God is stingy and stubborn? Why or why not?

Does this parable mean we should keep praying until God gives us what we want? Why or why not?

In your own words, what is the meaning of the parable?

NEW RHYTHMS FOR PRAYER

Prayer in practice is simply talking to God. You don't need to make it more complicated than that. Prayer is the act by which you, like Adam and Eve peeking up from behind the bushes, say "Here I am" in response to God's calling your name. Prayer, through Jesus and by the Spirit, puts you in the open embrace of the Father who listens with love. You can kneel, stand, sit, or recline. You can clasp your hands or lift them. You can bow your head or raise it to heaven. You can close your eyes or behold creation. You can pray aloud or in your head. However you go about it, all of it is *talking to God*.

I think once we realize prayer is simply talking to God it seems easier to do. But there are still many of us who have trouble finding our own

"The very thing we are allergic to—our helplessness—is what makes prayer work. It works because we are helpless."
—Paul Miller[27]

Bill Hybels' exceedingly readable and helpful *Too Busy Not To Pray* is a call to see prayer as absolute necessity. This book will encourage you in your prayer life without heaping guilt on you.

Though you might not come from a liturgical tradition, you still might enjoy reading through *The Book of Common Prayer*. It contains written prayers for most occasions, and can be helpful in putting words to what's going on in your heart during specific moments.

pace in the rhythm of intentional prayer. Below are some exercises that may or may not be new to you, but nevertheless may help you pick up the rhythm of prayer that, once begun, can take on a (prayer) life of their own in your daily abiding in Jesus.

Praying Written Prayers

Sometimes words are hard to find. Or after they've come, you find it frustrating to repeat yourself. If your prayers feel "stale," you may be interested in praying words written by others. This practice can be done in a rote and faithless manner, but many times praying pre-written prayers helps you find new ways to converse with God, reminds you of things you hadn't thought to pray for, or leads you to discover your own words on similar subjects. There's nothing magical or mystical about praying pre-written prayers, but neither is there anything shameful or remedial in it. Reading written prayers to God can be a great help for those who struggle with a wandering mind or the ability to articulate well.

There are numerous devotional and prayer books available that can help in this regard. One of the best is *The Valley of Vision*, a classic work of Puritan prayers and devotions, all of which are drenched in kingdom focus and centered on God's glory. (Of course, with written prayers you will need to be discerning about theological and spiritual content, as well as about whether the feelings expressed authentically apply to you. But then, those are discernments you must make in prayers you speak and write yourself.)

Praying Scripture

If written prayers seem like your kind of thing, there's no better source than the Word of God itself. The Psalms run the gamut of the human experience and are the likeliest place to find heartfelt, God-exalting prayers. But any Scripture can be prayed if you think through applying it prayerfully as part of the rhythm of feeling Scripture.

Wandering Prayer

The great thing about our God is that He takes you as you are but doesn't leave you as He finds you. This means that a wandering mind (and even body) is OK in prayer. If you're engaged in the practice of intentional prayer in solitude and quiet, God—who is outside of time— is not offended if it takes you awhile to get everything expressed, or you have to wander around your house, neighborhood, or park to clear yourself of noise. There's nothing magical about staying in one place or staying mentally on one track. You may begin with many words and slowly run out, but if you're drawing close to God, stay there and think.

"Our obsessive drive to control our minds in the presence of God, that is, to pray about one thing or stick to one list, may be a form of hiding from God."
—David Hansen[28]

Prayer: Finding the Heart's True Home, an extensive resource by Richard Foster, details all different sorts of prayers. It also leads you into these varied methods of praying, all while keeping the mystery in tact of what it means to speak to God.

Let your mind wander and then find its way back to prayer. There's no such thing as perfect prayer. Fortunately, Jesus is perfect, and He bears the burden of perfection in prayer for you. Walk around. Sing. Read. Intersperse prayer with devotional reading or Bible study. Talk to yourself a bit. Work out the kinks. It's OK. God can handle "messy."

Journaling Prayer

If you have trouble staying focused and want help with staying on track, one of the best practices to engage in is writing down your prayers instead of verbalizing them. This can keep you on track. And it has the added benefit of you being able to look back and see snapshots of your devotional life over time.

Many times even as we unplug from the noise of life, find a place of quiet solitude, and engage in prayer, we still have difficulty achieving rhythm in prayer because we're attempting a form that feels artificial or forced. Written prayers, scriptural prayers, wandering prayers, and journaled prayers are all ways to breathe new life into our time of intentional prayer. Perhaps the newness of one of these ways or the alternating of a variety of these ways can help us regain the rhythm of intimate conversation with God.

Which of these practices seems most appealing to you? Why?

What are some other fresh approaches to prayer that can be done in the quiet and solitude of intentional prayer time?

THE GOSPEL OF PRAYER

"In Jesus' name, amen."

I bet you've ended your prayers with that phrase many times. So what does it mean? Is it just a spiritual way to "sign off" from prayer, a way of saying "Sincerely" or "Yours truly"? What does it mean to pray in Jesus' name?

> "My longings are best met when, in prayer, I simply let my heart beat in time with the Lord's."
> —Joni Eareckson Tada[29]

I've experienced no greater motivation in intentional prayer than encountering the incredible fact that Jesus Christ is personally bearing my prayers to the throne room of Father God Almighty.

First Timothy 2:5 tells us, "For there is one God and one mediator between God and man, a man, Christ Jesus." This means that Jesus bridges the gap our sin creates between us and God. Sin encompasses not only our behavior but also our natural separation from God. On the other hand, Jesus' atoning work satisfies the penalty of sin and reconciles us to God. Do you see the miracle? Jesus' intervention covers even our weak and unprayed prayers.

I'm not making this up.

Not only does Christ's sufficiency cover the insufficiency of our prayer lives, He Himself is praying for us. Take a look at Hebrews 7:25:

"Therefore He is always able to save those who come to God through Him, since He always lives to intercede for them."

If you read the first few chapters of Hebrews, you get a sense of the cosmic importance of Jesus. The author, whose identity remains a mystery, was trying to point out the absolute pre-eminence of Jesus. He's better than the angels. He's better than Moses. And He's better than all the sacrifices.

Jesus' sacrifice, resurrection, and exaltation mediate salvation to us, and also sustain that salvation. He is always interceding for us. His work is an eternal prayer to God on our behalf, and if the prayer of a righteous man is very powerful (James 5:16), then the prayer of Jesus, the very righteousness of God incarnate in man, is all-powerful.

But wait, it gets better.

Can't think of how to pray, when to pray, or what to pray for? The Holy Spirit has you covered just as the Son does. In Romans 8:26 Paul wrote:

"In the same way the Spirit also joins to help in our weakness, because we do not know what to pray for as we should, but the Spirit Himself intercedes for us with unspoken groanings."

"Jesus isn't just the Savior of my soul. He's also the Savior of my prayers."
—Paul Miller[30]

There is no cause for frustration, guilt, or shame in prayer. The good news is that our Father loves us and knows our weaknesses. He sees our hearts, whether they're inclined to Him or not. And the gospel tells us that Christ died for hearts not inclined toward Him. Now that we're reconciled to the Father despite our sin, the Son and the Spirit pray for us even still, pleading the blood of Christ on our behalf for all time.

The gospel of prayer tells us that we don't pray to earn favor with God; we pray to enjoy God's favor already given to us in Jesus. In prayer, that favor is manifested through the Trinity praying within itself about and for us. It's staggering to consider that even now, in our weak, faithless, stumbling attempts at prayer, there is an internal conversation between the Father, Son, and Spirit about and for us.

That fact doesn't instill guilt; it creates rhythm.

What affect does knowing the Son and the Spirit pray for you have on your thoughts and attitudes about prayer?

Does knowing this good news make intentional prayer more or less appealing? Why?

What is the affect of the gospel of prayer on the practice of "abiding in Christ"?

How might the gospel of prayer apply to finding the rhythm of prayer?

"When praying makes you feel guilty, pretty soon you stop praying."
—Bill Hybels[31]

At your meeting time this week, watch the video called "Noise." As you do, consider how noisy your own life is. Aren't you ready for a little quiet?

A CLOSING PRAYER

"O God of the open ear, teach me to live by prayer as well as by providence, for myself, soul, body, children, family, church; give me a heart frameable to thy will; so might I live in prayer and honour thee, being kept from evil, known and unknown. Help me to see the sin that accompanies all I do, and the good I can distill from everything. Let me know that the work of prayer is to bring my will to thine, and that without this it is folly to pray.

"Teach me that it is wisdom for me to pray for all I have, out of love, willingly, not of necessity; that I may come to thee at any time, to lay open my needs acceptably to thee; that my great sin lies in my not keeping the savour of thy ways; that the remembrance of this truth is one way to the sense of thy presence; that there is no wrath like the wrath of being governed by my own lusts for my own ends."

—Taken from *The Valley of Vision*[32]

GET RHYTHM

In an effort to get rhythm this week, spend some time outside. Look at the trees, the water, and the wildlife around you. What rhythms can you isolate? Which ones do you see? Which ones do you hear? Use the space in the following pages to journal about your experience.

RHYTHM PRACTICE

Find a local prayer garden to visit, perhaps on the grounds of a church or hospital. Take some friends with you and spend time as individuals praying. Then pray as a group. Use the space in the following pages to journal about your experience.

RHYTHM THREE
PURPOSEFUL FASTING

The kingdom of God runs counter to the way of the world. So when Jesus said, "Deny yourself," the denial He was talking about, ironically, is about being filled. The consumer world that invites us to gorge ourselves daily on food, news, entertainment, sex, drugs, alcohol, work, reputation, notoriety, money, and all sorts of other things is really just inviting us to be satisfied with anything other than Jesus.

The problem with the suburbs isn't necessarily that everything is convenient, comfortable, and casual, but that routinely swimming in these things acclimates us to convenience, comfort, and casualness. None of those attributes are conducive to the life of discipleship that is abiding in Christ. Following Jesus just isn't convenient, comfortable, or casual—it's crucifixion. And this is why too many Christians have opted for a safer faith, complete with safer churches specializing in a safer gospel. The pursuit of the American dream has taken over the pursuit of God.

In John 6, the crowds loved it when Jesus handed out fish and chips, but once He started talking about subsisting on His body and blood, they scrammed. When Jesus later asked His disciples if they wanted to take off as well, Peter responded, "Lord, who will we go to?" (John 6:67-68). These days many might answer, "Well, Bed Bath & Beyond is having its white sale right now …"

In a world whose *modus operandi* is conspicuous consumption, going without can look downright weird if not outright ridiculous. Living the kingdom of God in a suburban culture is a call to simplicity in the land of the super-sized. While suburbia calls us to bigger, better, and more, the gospel of the kingdom leads us to empty ourselves, finding fulfillment in foregoing.

FASTING ISN'T ABOUT FOOD

If you have any experience with fasting, it's likely in the realm of food. Or perhaps you've given up something like coffee or the Internet for Lent. But fasting isn't exclusively about food. Nor is it meant to be only temporary in nature. Fasting is about giving up things by choice as part of an entire lifestyle *for the purpose of greater fulfillment.*

Very few of us ever have to go without things we need, and most of us rarely go without things we want. Nevertheless, when we do go without something it's typically the latest gadget or trinket we've decided we can't afford. In those instances, we aren't really fasting because we still want the thing but have decided we *can't* have it. This sort of "fasting" may prevent us from buying the $300 video game console or new pair of shoes, but it isn't an act of worship. It's an act of reason based on the figure in our bank account. Our affections are still with the item even if its enjoyment is not with us.

Fasting isn't really about food for the same reason it's not about not buying the next cool thing. There's nothing wrong with food or iPods or video games or shoes. Our desire for these things and our need to fast from them doesn't mean they're tainted or sinful in themselves; rather, our desire and need to fast means that *we* are tainted and sinful.

Is gluttony a sin because food is evil? Is pornography sinful because sex is bad? No, gluttony and pornography are wrong because they take good things and make them "god" things. Those distortions cause us to place hope in food, sex, or anything other than God for fulfillment. They try to satisfy desires they weren't meant to satisfy.

As a result, we look to food, drink, sex, and money for the answer to loneliness, depression, angst, discouragement, and the meaning of life, ascribing more worth to those things than they deserve. Gluttony and pornography (and most other sins) take God's good creation and make it the center of idolatrous religion.

Think about the sin in your own life. Which needs are you seeking to meet using a distorted version of a gift from God?

In *A Hunger For God*, John Piper points out that fasting isn't the end but the means to an end. When we fast, we seek greater satisfaction and pleasure in God. Fasting is the means by which we wean ourselves off of lesser pleasures.

"The human heart is a perpetual idol-factory."
— John Calvin[33]

How is that particular sin a type of idolatry?

Just like food and sex, suburbs aren't bad, and people aren't outside of God's will just because they live there. But the values and appetites characterized by suburbia are often the result of taking good things and making them god things, seeking fulfillment of needs in all the goods and services the consumer world has to offer. This idolatry is the root of alcoholism, drug addiction, pornography, greed, and more culturally acceptable sins like gluttony, materialism, and "retail therapy."

The religious architecture of this idolatry crosses the line between merely consuming goods and services (which is itself a neutral act) and consuming goods and services in appeasement of spiritual or emotional appetites. Idolatrous consumption feeds the consumer culture, and we slowly but surely find ourselves not only buying products but also buying the promises the products make.

The culture of consumerism appeals to our spiritual senses, and when our spiritual senses are engaged, we buy in. Whatever gets most of your energy, thoughts, and desire—that is your god. And if that's true, then fasting for most of us doesn't mean going without chocolate for a month—it means assassinating our idols.

As Jesus outlined the blueprint of the kingdom in the Sermon on the Mount, He cut to the heart of this very issue with laser-like precision:

"Don't collect for yourselves treasures on earth, where moth and rust destroy and where thieves break in and steal. But collect for yourselves treasures in heaven, where neither moth nor rust destroys, and where thieves don't break in and steal. For where your treasure is, there your heart will be also" (Matthew 6:19-21).

Jesus pulls the façade off the silliness of idolatry. It is utter foolishness because its treasures are temporary. Your house may be awesome but it can burn to the ground. Your car may be fancy but it's going to rust. Your cell phone may let you track the progress of the lunar rover but your cell phone (and the lunar rover) can be stolen. And yet we treat these things with the reverence befitting a permanence they do not have. We pour our thoughts, physical energy, emotions, hopes, and

Today, the worldwide revenues of the pornography industry equal more than the revenues of the top technology companies—Microsoft, Google, Amazon, eBay, Yahoo!, Apple, Netflix and EarthLink—combined.[34]

Did you know that the phrase "bad breath" was unknown in popular culture until Listerine was invented?[35]

A newspaper reader as early as 1897 remarked that people once "skipped ads unless some want compelled us to read, while now we read to find out what we really want."[36]

lots and lots of our finances into things that will break down, fall apart, get stolen, or be obsolete in a year.

Instead, Jesus commanded those who abide in His kingdom to treasure permanent things—things with eternal value. And then He honed in on the root of all of our consumeristic dysfunction: idolatry.

"For where your treasure is, there your heart will be also."

Whatever you treasure possesses your heart.

What are some treasures you can lay up in heaven?

What does it mean that your heart is where your treasure is?

What heart/treasure issue do you struggle with the most?

What would you like to fast from in order to win that spiritual battle?

THE IMPORTANCE OF ENOUGH

Our failure to fast from crass consumerism stems from our failure to say "enough!" For those hooked on the drugs of materialism and consumption, there is no such thing as enough. Instead, our mantra is "more!" a command that by definition cannot be satisfied.

Fasting from anything is a sign that we're denying "more" and saying "enough."

But as we've just learned, we have trouble saying "enough" in the first place because of the appetites of our flesh and desires of our hearts.

"The dilemma posed by consumerism is not the endless manufacturing of desires, but the temptation to settle for desires far below what we were created for."
—Skye Jethani[37]

Americans seem to be incapable of saying "enough." The national debt continues to tick upward, and each person's share is somewhere around $40,000.[38]

Just because we fast from things that don't satisfy our spiritual senses doesn't mean we've tamed our senses or that they somehow go into hibernation. In order to truly say "enough" we have to experience satisfaction of our spiritual senses. So we must not only practice the self-denial of fasting; something has to step in to take the place of whatever we're fasting from. And the only satisfaction that truly satisfies is Jesus Christ Himself.

Return to the Beatitudes at the front of the Sermon on the Mount in Matthew 5:3-11. These declarations are the promises of the "enough" that is available for those who abide in the kingdom of God.

What are the needs and desires addressed in the Beatitudes?

What are the satisfactions provided in God's kingdom?

In the middle of the Beatitudes we find this tenet of the kingdom:

"Blessed are those who hunger and thirst for righteousness, because they will be filled" (v. 6).

Until we hunger and thirst for God we will never truly be fulfilled. Only He can satisfy our inward groaning for righteousness. Psalm 42:1 speaks to this perfect fit, as David cries:

"As a deer longs for streams of water, so I long for You, God."

But instead of taking that inner thirst to the living water of God, we turn to the toxic sludge of whatever is offered outside the kingdom. We see that verse and don't see our means to assassinating idols but something nice to slap on a coffee mug below a picture of a deer and sell for $9.95 at the Christian bookstore.

This hunger and thirst for righteousness, this panting of our souls for water is a description of our longing for something bigger and better—for the divine metronome that has set the tick-tock of our insides. In

"He is no fool who gives what he cannot keep to gain that which he cannot lose."
—Jim Eliot[39]

In John 4, Jesus encountered a woman who sought "more" in the odd coupling of sexual relationships and theological debates. He offered her Himself instead, saying that He is "living water," a drink from which would end her thirst forever.

short, we are instruments aching from artificial beats, longing for true spiritual rhythms.

Fasting is one of these rhythms, and it's a crucial one because it involves repenting from the weight of all that slows us down. Fasting is a rhythm in the same way not fasting is a rhythm. It's the way we live in service to something outside of ourselves. Big houses and fancy cars aren't necessarily bad things, but orienting our lives around paying for, building, and maintaining those things can be. Think about it—we make all kinds of financial, time, and emotional sacrifices for that stuff. The rhythms of our lives already portray our willingness to go without things like wise financial management, time to rest, anonymity, and sometimes even our good health in order to get what we want. And those sacrifices are senseless. All the rhythm of fasting asks us to do is sacrifice for better, permanent, more fulfilling things.

The late comedian George Carlin was an angry guy who mocked the very idea of God, but even he understood the superficial fulfillment of consumerism. One of his most famous routines involved the relation of the American dream to "stuff." Carlin mused that we buy a home so that our stuff will fit in it, but then proceed to "need" a bigger home because our accumulation of stuff doesn't end. According to him, all a house is used for is a place to hold your stuff while you're out getting more stuff. Even the biggest house is not big enough to contain the fruit of conspicuous consumption.

Meanwhile Jesus draws near and—ready to rebuke materialism (Luke 12:33) and rescue the weary (Matthew 11:28)—He stands over us with arms outstretched. To all of us moving to the rhythm of "more" He shouts "enough!"

How serious a problem is the rhythm of "more" in your life?

What is the biggest difficulty for you in living the rhythm of "enough"?

How do you plan to reduce or eliminate this difficulty?

Jeremiah 2:13 reveals two sins of God's people that pertain to the subject of fasting. According to that verse, the people had "abandoned Me, the fountain of living water, and dug cisterns for themselves, cracked cisterns that cannot hold water." These cracked cisterns are our efforts to find our completeness and wholeness in anything except God.

"My grace is sufficient for you" (2 Corinthians 12:9).

FALSE FASTING

We must return to the difference between "doing" and "being" now, because the temptation we face in reading the Beatitudes and the rest of the Sermon on the Mount is to put on behavioral expectations like a costume and play a religious part without undergoing any heart change at all. Jesus called us out on this when He spoke specifically about fasting in the Sermon:

"Whenever you fast, don't be sad-faced like the hypocrites. For they make their faces unattractive so their fasting is obvious to people. I assure you: They've got their reward! But when you fast, put oil on your head, and wash your face, so that you don't show your fasting to people but to your Father who is in secret. And your Father who sees in secret will reward you" (Matthew 6:16-18).

Jesus warned against behavioral alignment with the kingdom that lacks heart alignment. Acting humbly is not the same as *being* humble.

This is a powerful truth. When we skim over it, it seems reasonable enough. None of us like hypocritical people, and none of us want to be one of those people. But the way Jesus commanded humble fasting cuts right to the heart of pretense. He actually encouraged "keeping up appearances" as a means of not keeping up appearances. Isn't that weird?

In classical Greek, the noun *hypocrite* has its roots in performance arts and simply means "actor."

The well-appointed gated communities of suburbia might be a fitting metaphor for the Pharisees of Jesus' day. He called them "whitewashed tombs" (Matthew 23:27)—pretty on the outside but rotten on the inside. We know that nice suburban neighborhoods are not shelters from sin and brokenness; those who live there take that stuff with them inside their gates and hearts. No amount of landscaping and architectural lighting can gussy up infidelity, addiction, abuse, extortion, divorce, depression, and anger.

Yet in Matthew 6:16-18 Jesus told those who fast to clean themselves up a bit: Fix your hair, shave, put on some deodorant. Why? Because trying to look like you're fasting is as fake as trying to look like you have it all together. The difference is not appearance but attitude. The difference is the heart.

"We gravitate toward the trite and trivial rather than the somber and grave, and we pride ourselves on adornment and complexity rather than simplicity, often because many of us are trying desperately to hide our true selves."

—Gary Thomas[40]

If studying this book and trying to resemble what it suggests is just an exercise in looking more spiritual, you're missing the point. The whole point of abiding in Christ according to the rhythms of the kingdom is that life is found outside of your efforts and that the rhythms don't originate with you. You can study your Bible, pray, fast, give to charity, and go to church all you want, but if it's not the work of a heart bent toward God, the prophet Isaiah calls it "filthy rags" (Isaiah 64:6, NIV).

The New Testament church at various times had to ward off the infiltration of a group of heretics called ascetics. Ascetics abstained from certain food or drink, disengaged from the wider culture, and adopted rigorous religious disciplines in pursuit of transcendence, enlightenment, or holiness. For these guys, fasting was the end, not a means to the end. Ascetics trusted their own works to merit salvation.

Joyful fasting is not about asceticism. It's not about becoming a hermit or a hippie. Many times in Christian critiques of suburban life, followers of Jesus are urged to believe they can't be fruitful in suburbia, that somehow rural areas are naturally more conducive to spiritual growth. This sort of asceticism looks down on urban and suburban dwellers and thinks of them as lesser Christians because of their position or possessions. But someone proud of his lack may well be in deeper sin than someone content with his abundance.

No, fasting is not about performance, to impress God or others. Fasting is a posture. It's a posture of denial we take toward the consumer offerings of the world and of submission to the loving care and provision of God.

Why is it so tempting to wear our spiritual accomplishments on our sleeves?

What are some ways a spirit of pride can corrupt the spiritual disciplines of Bible study, prayer, fasting, etc.?

What did Jesus mean in Matthew 6:16 when He said of the hypocritical fasters, "They've got their reward"?

Paul's letter to the Colossians, for instance, offers instruction in response to the threat of self-righteous asceticism.

"These people honor Me with their lips, but their heart is far from Me" (Matthew 15:8).

TRUE FASTING

This kingdom rhythm is called "purposeful fasting" because we're after something more than just self-denial. If we're weaning ourselves off of the wares of the world, where do we draw worth? Where do we place our hopes? What entertains our hearts? If it's not movies, television, the Web, food, drink, or shopping, then what's left?

Joy is left. And true fasting results in joy for one primary reason: *it is worship of God.*

We're tempted to let everyone know we're fasting, broadcasting from the rooftops that we don't have cable or that we only buy from Goodwill, because we aren't worshiping God so much as seeking the religious admiration of others. False fasting stems even from pleasant hypocrisy and polite self-righteousness; it doesn't have to be "mean" like the Pharisees'. But looking for the strength to fast from others' admiration or approval or even our own good feeling and self-satisfaction over righteous accomplishments will not work out. That well dries up. If we fast like that, we'll eventually become bitter over all we think we're missing out on.

"Do not grieve, because your strength comes from rejoicing in the LORD" (Nehemiah 8:10b).

But a heart tuned to God, drawing strength from Him, will have what it takes to self-deny. When fasting is an act of worship, practiced as a regular rhythm of life in Christ's kingdom, the Spirit of worship sustains us, a peace that is beyond understanding overcomes us, and a joy unspeakable flows from us.

We don't live in a world where self-denial is encouraged. I've heard maturity defined as "the ability to delay gratification." If that's true, consumer culture is itself immature and designed to cultivate immaturity. A daily perusal of Twitter and Facebook updates reveals the complaints of friends and family (and myself) when the drive-thru line is long, when the lady in front of us at the checkout digs in her purse for her billfold at the last second, when the airline doesn't serve a meal on a lunchtime flight, and when the DVR cuts off the end of our favorite shows. In none of these petty irritations is the economy of eternity. There is no joy of not getting what we want.

"You love Him, though you have not seen Him. And though not seeing Him now, you believe in Him and rejoice with inexpressible and glorious joy" (1 Peter 1:8).

It's in this world of imaginary problems that the cross of Christ seems foolish. It's foolishness because the cross is the very emblem of self-denial, self-emptying, and self-sacrifice. The cross is the polar opposite of the heartfelt wrath we feel when someone takes our parking space. But the cross is, however, the symbol of kingdom fasting—*purposeful fasting for the sake of joy.*

The author of Hebrews framed it this way:

"Therefore since we also have such a large cloud of witnesses surrounding us, let us lay aside every weight and the sin that so easily ensnares us, and run with endurance the race that lies before us, keeping our eyes on Jesus, the source and perfecter of our faith, who for the joy that lay before Him endured a cross and despised the shame, and has sat down at the right hand of God's throne" (Hebrews 12:1-2).

This passage tells us that Jesus endured the cross "for the joy that lay before Him." He didn't see the sort of gratification in the cross many of us see in the golden arches or the little green mermaid (or whatever the Starbucks logo is). He saw the gratification of joy beyond the cross, and the cross as the means to the joy of renewed intimacy with the Father ("at the right hand of God's throne").

> **What instructions might you draw from this passage about finding rhythm in the Christian life? What is required? What is gained?**

> **What does it mean that Jesus "despised the shame" of the cross?**

FEASTING

The original sin centered on fasting and feasting. Adam and Eve were allowed to eat of anything they wanted in the garden of Eden, with one exception. Just one tree was off limits. The commanded fast was very specific and the permitted feast was everywhere else. But Satan knew how to bait the hook. Take a look at Genesis 3:1-6:

"Now the serpent was the most cunning of all the wild animals that the Lord God had made. He said to the woman, 'Did God really say, "You can't eat from any tree in the garden"?'

"The woman said to the serpent, 'We may eat the fruit from the trees in the garden. But about the fruit of the tree in the middle of the garden, God said, "You must not eat it or touch it, or you will die."'

It's worth noting in this passage that the author urged us to throw off two things: both sin and anything else that might entangle us. That leads us to the knowledge that there are things in our lives that aren't inherently sinful but nonetheless hold us back in our pursuit of Christ.

"All divine life, and all the precious fruits of it, pardon, peace and holiness, spring from the cross."
—John Berridge[41]

"'No! You will not die,' the serpent said to the woman. 'In fact, God knows that when you eat it your eyes will be opened and you will be like God, knowing good and evil.'

"Then the woman saw that the tree was good for food and delightful to look at, and that it was desirable for obtaining wisdom. So she took some of its fruit and ate it; she also gave some to her husband, who was with her, and he ate it."

This interaction is the template for all temptation throughout history. We see in Eve's final submission the very DNA of original sin. The lures then are the same as today's. Look in the last verse again: She saw that it was good for food, that it looked pretty, and that it would benefit her in some way. John the apostle summed up the essence of worldliness this way:

"Do not love the world or the things that belong to the world. If anyone loves the world, love for the Father is not in him. Because everything that belongs to the world—the lust of the flesh, the lust of the eyes, and the pride in one's lifestyle—is not from the Father, but is from the world" (1 John 2:15-16).

John labeled the allure of self-fulfillment as "everything that belongs to the world." If this were a can of soup on the grocery store shelf, the ingredients on the back would read: lust of the flesh, lust of the eyes, and pride.

These three ingredients are in Eve's denial of "enough" and pursuit of "more." She saw the fruit would be good for food, giving in to the appetite of her flesh. She saw that it looked pretty, giving in to the lust of her eyes. And she thought it would make her like God, giving in to the temptation of pride.

These are the three ingredients at work any time we trade "enough" for "more." Take our supposed need for technology as an example. Each new gadget appeals to our appetite for accumulation. New gadgets look shiny. New gadgets promise connection, advancement, coolness. And so will the next one that is released.

> **Consider again your own appetite for "more." How do you see these three elements at work in the specific things you want more of?**

Listen to "Satisfaction," an audio devotion from author Jared C. Wilson. Your group leader can send it to you via e-mail. As you listen, consider what exactly you are feasting on.

"Doesn't the ear test words as the palate tastes food?" (Job 34:3).

Apple is a master of this sort of strategy. Consider the technology of the iPod. When there is a new version released (about every 18 months), Apple ceases production of the next oldest model, forcing the consumer to buy the new one. It's translated into a felt need of having the newest gadget since the slightly older one isn't even in production any more.

The good news is that we have both the power to fast from idols and the forgiveness to receive for when we don't. Jesus Christ healed the brokenness set loose by Adam and Eve in the garden by undergoing the same temptation to feast on the world's wares.

"Then Jesus was led up by the Spirit into the wilderness to be tempted by the Devil. After He had fasted 40 days and 40 nights, He was hungry. Then the tempter approached Him and said, 'If You are the Son of God, tell these stones to become bread.'

"But He answered, 'It is written: Man must not live on bread alone but on every word that comes from the mouth of God.'

"Then the Devil took Him to the holy city, had Him stand on the pinnacle of the temple, and said to Him, 'If You are the Son of God, throw Yourself down. For it is written: He will give His angels orders concerning you and, they will support you with their hands so that you will not strike your foot against a stone.'

"Jesus told him, 'It is also written: Do not test the Lord your God.'

"Again, the Devil took Him to a very high mountain and showed Him all the kingdoms of the world and their splendor. And he said to Him, 'I will give You all these things if You will fall down and worship me.'

"Then Jesus told him, 'Go away, Satan! For it is written: Worship the Lord your God, and serve only Him'" (Matthew 4:1-10).

The first practical thing we see in this passage is that Jesus didn't run out of the "It is written" statements as Eve had. For every twisting of God's words Satan could present, Jesus had the Word of God at the ready to counterstrike. Eve was only able to correct Satan once. The practical application is this: Don't run out of Scripture. You won't be able to say "no thanks" to everything that belongs to the world if you aren't already full. People who say "more" don't yet feel "enough." It's easier to fast joyfully if we are feasting on the revelation of God.

> **What does Jesus say in Matthew 4:1-10 about what we live on? How does that relate to the rhythm of feeling Scripture?**

"This is that glory of Christ whereof one view will scatter all the fears, answer all the objections, and disperse all the depressions of poor, tempted, doubting souls; to all believers it is an anchor which they may cast within the veil, to hold them firm and steadfast in all trials, storms and temptations, both in life and in death."
—John Owen[42]

How does what Jesus said relate to the request for daily bread in the Lord's Prayer?

List the three temptations facing Jesus in this passage. Then label them accordingly: lust of flesh (appetites); lust of eyes; pride.

"The one who eats My flesh and drinks My blood lives in Me, and I in him" (John 6:56).

How important is it that Jesus did what Eve and Adam didn't? Why?

SEEKING SIMPLICITY

Feasting on the Scriptures and Christ Himself prepares us to joyfully fast from the promises of fulfillment made by our consumer culture. When we get the hang of this practice, we are walking in yet another kingdom rhythm—the outward effects of life in Christ. This may look "weird." The rhythm of purposeful fasting often produces a life of simplicity—intentional, strategic simplicity.

"The practice of fasting goes together with this teaching about nourishing ourselves on the person of Jesus."
—Dallas Willard[43]

Musician and Compassion International advocate Shaun Groves has written many times about the fruitfulness of purposeful fasting. After experiencing the comforts provided by a successful music career and the conveniences of suburban Nashville, Tennessee, Shaun went on a Compassion "vision trip" to the slums of El Salvador and had his world "wrecked." At the end of the trip, before the flight home, the American visitors gathered to share their feelings about their experience. Shaun wrote:

"When it was my turn to talk about my feelings all I felt was insignificance and so I vomited that emotion up everywhere. (With a lot more words) I said I just didn't care anymore.

"About what? About what color we paint the den. About whether my song is climbing the charts. About who the president is. About the gig next week. About what kind of cheese I can get on my Subway sandwich. About seeing that new movie. About that new laptop I wanted. About telling the interviewer what kind of animal I'd like to be. About mowing the yard.

"I just didn't care anymore. It didn't feel significant—none of it—not standing back to back with feeding kids, teaching them to read, giving them life-saving medicine, teaching their moms how to sew, telling them they matter to God and to me. Nothing in my whole life back home seemed as significant as my week in El Salvador with Compassion International. Nothing."[45]

Sometimes it's difficult to imagine a lifestyle of fasting until you actually encounter those who have no choice but to fast. It can certainly take the shine off every metal object in every glossy-paged magazine.

You can read more about how Shaun Groves and his family cultivated simplicity in their lives by visiting *shaungroves.com/2008/05/simplifying-simplicity-part-2/.*

Shaun Groves said "enough" to "more." So he and his family sold their big house and downsized, not because their income decreased or because their family shrunk, but simply because they wanted to have more to give away. After that huge first step, they worked diligently to create more simplicity in their lives, bringing purposeful fasting to bear in more and more areas of their finances and lifestyle.

Do Shaun and millions of others walk in the rhythm of purposeful fasting like this to declare how awesome they are? No, they do it because they have tasted the "enough" of the gospel of the kingdom and because they want others to as well. And it's hard to convince others of the goodness of the kingdom of God when we can't seem to live without the "goodness" of the world.

Purposeful fasting creates a culture of simplicity in our lives and the life of our churches, and that simplicity gives us the energy, money, and available time to minister to others. Joyful fasting enables us to live out the Beatitudes for those the Beatitudes addresses. Here's what God says about this in Isaiah 58:5-7:

"Will the fast I choose be like this:
A day for a person to deny himself,
to bow his head like a reed,
and to spread out sackcloth and ashes?
Will you call this a fast
and a day acceptable to the Lord?

"Isn't the fast I choose:
To break the chains of wickedness,
to untie the ropes of the yoke,
to set the oppressed free,
and to tear off every yoke?

"Is it not to share your bread with the hungry,
to bring the poor and homeless into your house,
to clothe the naked when you see him,
and to not ignore your own flesh and blood?"

What sort of fasting does God say to avoid?

What is the purpose of fasting, according to God?

"Pure and undefiled religion before our God and Father is this: to look after orphans and widows in their distress and to keep oneself unstained by the world" (James 1:27).

Practically speaking, how does fasting lead to justice? Provide some specific ideas and examples.

Leviticus 19 gives a command to those harvesting in their fields. It says they shouldn't reap all the way to the edges or go back and pick up the leftovers. Instead, they should leave what's left for those who don't have enough to eat. This concept of intentional margin can be applied not only to fields, but to our calendars, finances, and time.

Have you heard of the concept of "margin"? Most of us don't have much margin in our lives. Our schedules are filled to the brim with work, school, church, entertainment, and other obligations and diversions. There's not much time left over for God or others. Many of us don't have much financial margin either. We expand our expenses to the limits of our income, we creep deeper into debt, and we don't save or give much. Yet the simplicity created by purposeful fasting provides margin. Room to breathe. And in that (hopefully ever-increasing) margin, we're able to first look up from ourselves and *notice* our neighbor, and then love him as we do ourselves. That's what we'll explore in our next session.

A CLOSING PRAYER

"Grant, most sweet and loving Jesus, that I may seek my repose in You above every creature; above all health and beauty; above every honor and glory; every power and dignity; above all knowledge and cleverness, all riches and arts, all joy and gladness; above all fame and praise, all sweetness and consolation; above every hope and promise, every merit and desire; above all the gifts and favors that You can give or pour down upon me; above all joy and gladness; above all fame and praise, all sweetness and consolation; above every hope and promise, every merit and desire; above all the gifts and favors that You can give or pour down upon me; above all the joy and exultation that the mind can receive and feel; and finally, above the angels and archangels and all the heavenly host; above all things visible and invisible; and may I seek my repose in You above everything that is not You, my God.

"For you, O Lord my God, are above all things the best."

—Taken from *Imitation of Christ*[48]

GET RHYTHM

This week view some video clips from the Broadway musical "Stomp." Even if you've seen it before, you'll be amazed how the ordinary rhythms and instruments of life come together. Find clips on YouTube or by googling "Stomp." Use the space in the following pages to journal about what you observe.

RHYTHM PRACTICE

This week, fast from a common indulgence, practice, or entertainment. It might be Facebook, your MP3 player, television, or certain daily snacks. Use the space in the following pages to journal about your experience.

RHYTHM THREE ABIDE

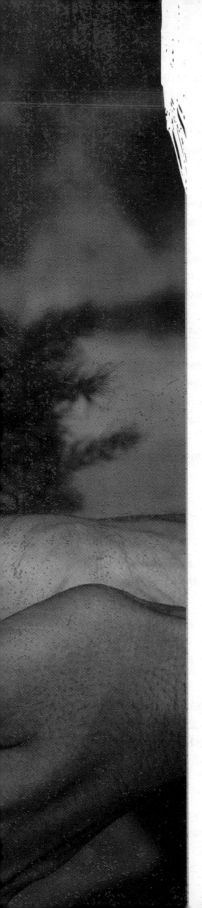

RHYTHM FOUR
JOYFUL SERVICE

One of the sad ironies of the suburbs is how close in proximity everyone is despite the intentional effort to maintain privacy and individualism. Our traffic is congested, our grocery stores are packed, our malls are busy—even our homes are sometimes only eight feet away from another on either side. Yet we do our best to mind our own business and see to it that everyone else minds theirs.

Suburban self-orientation kills the promise of relational connection. This modern tragedy affects nearly all aspects of social life, including spiritual ones. In his groundbreaking book *Bowling Alone,* psychologist Robert Putnam examines the detrimental effect of increased individualism and personal isolation even in congested urban and suburban areas. The title references that once-great American pastime: bowling. So long a staple of suburban communal recreation, bowling leagues and parties have decreased. More and more people are bowling alone.

Putnam argues that this development is merely reflective of the larger decrease in what he calls "social capital," the amassed connections between individual people and community groups that contribute to the overall health of both individuals and communities.[49]

We can see the "bowling alone" effect in our own neighborhoods. When I was a child (which was not that long ago, thank you very much) the neighborhood streets and yards were noisy with children riding bikes, playing tag or football, and the like. Neighborhood boys would play "army" in the woods. Girls would gather on curbs and sing songs. These days many suburban neighborhoods are eerily quiet. All the children are inside playing video games or surfing the Internet I suppose. By themselves.

GETTING OFF TRACK

To prove there is really nothing new under the sun (Ecclesiastes 1:9), take a look at what Mark Twain wrote in the late 1860's about New York City: "It is a splendid desert—a domed and steepled solitude, where the stranger is lonely in the midst of a million of his race."[50] Is there a better spiritual summing up of the city—or the suburbs—than a place where millions of people can be alone together?

But it's not just the suburbs or the city where loneliness is the norm. At the community breakfast I attended in rural Vermont the morning I wrote this chapter, one of the men challenged the "Yankee independence" of New Englanders. And rugged individualism is as American as apple pie (which we now buy in single servings from vending machines so we can—you guessed it—eat them by ourselves).

The consumer culture most of us live in says this situation is fine and dandy. It accommodates and affirms our self-centeredness, encouraging our inclination to think relationships and concern for others are overrated and unnecessary. If the Great Commandment is to love God with everything we've got and then to love our neighbors at least as much as we love ourselves, the vast majority of us have lots of repenting to do.

> **How do you see the "bowling alone" principle at work in your own community?**

> **Why do you think there is an increased tendency toward individual isolation? How do you think God feels about it?**

MEET BILL

Bill is 28 years old and lives in a condominium in a typical middle-class suburb of a mid-size city. He gets up at 6:30 every morning, shaves, showers, dresses, and eats breakfast. If he has time, he watches some cable news or surfs the Web. Forty-five minutes after waking, he leaves for work.

With his to-go cup full of coffee, Bill drives to the city via the interstate. It takes him an hour, sometimes a little more. He tried carpooling

Sixty percent of American commuting is suburb-related.[51]

"Just then, an expert in the law stood up to test him, saying, 'Teacher, what must I do to inherit eternal life?'

"'What is written in the law?' He asked him. 'How do you read it?'

"He answered: 'Love the Lord your God with all your heart, with all your soul, with all your strength, and with all your mind; and your neighbor as yourself.'

"'You've answered correctly,' He told him. 'Do this and you will live'" (Luke 10:25-28).

RHYTHM FOUR ABIDE

once, but he found the carpoolers unreliable, and he knows if he doesn't leave by 7:15 a.m. or so, the traffic will be much thicker and the commute much more frustrating.

Arriving at work around 8:15 a.m. (on a good day with no delays), Bill immediately heads to his cubicle. His coworkers are either too busy working or too busy waking up, so no one gives anybody else much more than a polite nod.

Bill spends four hours pushing numbers around spreadsheets and responding to e-mails. At lunch time, he walks down to the corner fast food joint, gets a value meal to go, and returns to his cubicle. Bill eats at his desk while surfing news sites and watching YouTube videos.

When lunch is over, Bill spends another four hours pushing numbers around and responding to e-mails. He gets a few breaks in this time, so he uses the restroom, gets a soda out of the machine in the break room, and plays games on Facebook. Every now and then someone will stop by his cubicle to say hey, chit-chat about sports, or ask about reports that are (or *were*) due.

At 5:15 p.m., Bill walks out to the parking garage. Some of his coworkers have already left, and the ones who remain are busy getting ready to go home, so no one keeps anybody from getting on the road. He gets in his car and begins the drive home, which takes longer than the morning commute.

Bill enters his neighborhood at 6:30 p.m., drives to the parking lot of his condo, takes his assigned space, and walks to his front door. He enters the house and turns on the TV. He is too tired to worry about dinner for the moment. At 8:00 p.m. he gets hungry, forages out a can of soup, gets it simmering, and makes a sandwich.

Bill goes to bed at 11:00 p.m., making sure his alarm is set for 6:30 a.m. When the morning comes, he does it all over again.

On Saturdays, Bill sometimes goes out, but he mostly stays in and watches movies, plays video games, noodles around on his guitar, and chats with friends on the Internet. On Sunday mornings, Bill goes to church, where he is greeted at the door but then talks to no one else. He sits in the same place every week, sings along to the music, usually enjoys the sermon, and goes home immediately after the closing prayer so he doesn't miss the start of the football game.

According to the Texas Transportation Institute, the average American will spend a full work week every year in traffic.[52]

Sound familiar? How is your daily routine like Bill's?

It is estimated that around 98 million people will watch the Super Bowl this year.[52]

What's appealing to you about living like that? What are the drawbacks?

Whether we want to admit it or not, our routines are a lot like Bill's. Maybe they're not quite as boring or predictable, but they might be just as lonely. Even if Bill were a little older, married with school-aged children, his interaction with them would still be limited because of his daily schedule, and his interaction with those outside his family would be even more limited.

Suburbia is great at getting us onto a track. We stay on our tracks daily, taking the same route. Bed to car, car to work, work to car, car to garage. The tracks are predictable and comfortable. We know what to expect. The only thing asked of us is that we go with the flow. But our tracks are actually ruts. And while we keep our heads down as we move within our ruts, people pass us on all sides, most of them in ruts of their own, and each of us becomes the proverbial island in the stream.

To read more about suburban rhythms and how they are infiltrating our lives, check out *Death by Suburb: How to Keep the Suburbs from Killing Your Soul* by David L. Goetz. In it, you'll learn even more practices counter to the lifestyle of suburbia.

This is the rhythm of suburbia. It is seductive in its self-centeredness.

If you agree that your life is fairly predictable, what does your rut look like?

How is that rhythm self-centered?

When John the Baptist and then Jesus began calling the world to attention, they preached, "Repent, for the kingdom of heaven has come near!" (Matthew 4:17). Jesus wanted to get people out of their ruts. That's essentially what "repent" means: Turn away from the way you're going and go a new way. That new way is the kingdom of God.

In our day, as in Jesus', the world's ruts are individualistic, consumeristic, self-centered, and self-concerned. Repentance, therefore, is an about-face from our way toward the self-crucifying way of Jesus. The call of the kingdom requires us to love our neighbors, and loving our neighbors begins with lifting our eyes to notice them. It continues by calling us to open our mouths to speak to them, open our homes to host them, open our arms to share with them, and open our hearts to care for them.

"Next to the blessed sacrament itself, your neighbor is the holiest object presented to your senses."
—C. S. Lewis[54]

Bill's life revolves around his own agenda, his own needs, and his own wants. Even his spiritual life is compartmentalized, neatly fit into the larger order of his lifestyle. Bill has arranged things to be as convenient as possible, and even when he has the inclination to "do hard things," he is usually too tired to do them. Bill is not often faced with the opportunity to serve or help others simply because he rarely makes time to interact with others in substantive ways. It's hard for him to be generous with others because he's generally generous with himself and thinks of others as window dressing in his life.

The rhythm of consumer culture not only encourages an ungenerous lifestyle, but it also rewards it. There's always something new or interesting to consume, and consuming takes time, money, and interest—the three things needed to be generous. The siren call of self-service and self-help comes from the spirit of consumer culture, which is dead set against generosity and service, because widespread generosity and service would be the death of that culture.

But we can adapt this culture to the advantage of the kingdom. The very design and structure of suburbia are ripe and ready to make the rhythms of generosity and service quite easy to adopt.

In a study sponsored by Ronald McDonald House Charities, 93 percent of Americans surveyed believe it's important to promote volunteerism. However, more than half (51 percent) said they'd rather read, watch TV, or visit the in-laws than volunteer for charity.[55]

Assuming you can't quit your job or move from where you live, what else might you do to get out of your rut?

How might life in suburbia actually be used to the advantage of the kingdom of God? What does suburbia have that can be "exploited" for the kingdom that other areas might not have?

"Personal salvation is too small a controlling story. Peter and Andrew did not 'get saved' and retreat to a vacation fishing village."
—Charlie Peacock[56]

To refresh your memory about the account of Sodom and Gomorrah, read Genesis 18–19.

AN OUTWARD FAITH

The American church has done a great disservice in merging one's journey of faith with the values of the American dream. We like to use phrases like "personal Lord and Savior" and "personal relationship with Jesus." Neither of these phrases is wrong per se, but neither reflects the fullness of life in Jesus' kingdom. The truth is that while we are saved as individuals, we are not saved to an individual walk. And while our faith may be personal, it is not private. Christianity isn't meant to occupy one time slot in the weekly programming of our lives.

After he'd murdered Abel, Cain was called out by God and asked about his brother's whereabouts. Cain responded defensively and dismissively: "Am I my brother's keeper?" (Genesis 4:9, NIV). Many of us ask the same question every day.

And though our actions shout "No!" to that question, the correct answer is unequivocally "Yes." We are the keepers of our brothers if we mean to abide in Christ. Some of us live as though we only need to avoid committing some gross sin, or at least not commit a sin that is grosser than anybody else's. But personal morality is not the point of the kingdom. Take a look at this revelation about the famous destruction of Sodom and Gomorrah:

"Now this was the iniquity of your sister Sodom: she and her daughters had pride, plenty of food, and comfortable security, but didn't support the poor and needy" (Ezekiel 16:49).

Despite all the sexual immorality and violence in Sodom, the sin God honed in on was the selfish neglect of the poor and needy by those who were comfortable and content. Does this sound like anybody you know?

In consumer culture, faith just becomes another add-on, customized and personalized for our own needs and tastes. We see this in everything from church programming to Christian product marketing.

We see the proof in our lives, which keeps us in the rut of self-tailored spirituality that is nonetheless barren of the fruit of the Spirit.

But faith in Christ, despite being an inward conviction, has outward manifestation, particularly in grace-driven connection to other people. If our faith is just an inward experience, it's fundamentally a self-help project. In such inward faith, Jesus is Dr. Phil or Dr. Drew, not the Lord of the universe or the Bridegroom of the church.

Consider the following Scriptures:

"In the same way, let your light shine before men, so that they may see your good works and give glory to your Father in heaven" (Matthew 5:16).

"For we are His creation—created in Christ Jesus for good works, which God prepared ahead of time so that we should walk in them" (Ephesians 2:10).

"Based on the gift they have received, everyone should use it to serve others, as good managers of the varied grace of God" (1 Peter 4:10).

What are the common elements of these three verses?

What two things does Ephesians 2:10 say about good works?

What do you think it means to "walk in them"?

KINGDOM CITIZENSHIP AND THE ALLEGIANCE OF LOVE

If our citizenship is first and foremost in the world we live, it makes very good sense to devote our allegiance to ourselves. We do live in a democracy, after all (or at least a representative republic). The power

"The cross isn't an accessory."
—Michael Horton[57]

"What God did to us, we then owed to others. The more we received, the more we were able to give."
—Dietrich Bonhoeffer[58]

In the six chapters of the Book of Ephesians, Paul used the Greek word for "walk" six times. In addition to advising that we walk in good works, he also wrote that we should walk in love, walk in a manner worthy of our calling to be Christ-followers, and walk in unity.

lies with the people, and our birthright is life, liberty, and the pursuit of happiness. But if my citizenship is first and foremost in the kingdom, all bets are off.

In John 3:3, Jesus blew the mind of a Pharisee, Nicodemus, by saying:

"I assure you: Unless someone is born again, he cannot see the kingdom of God."

The whole concept of being "born again" speaks to the resurrection-quality life Jesus brings through Himself. Basically Jesus was saying that to experience the kingdom, you have to be made truly alive for the first time. The whole notion of being born again speaks to new life, new identity, new status—new *everything*. Included in this "everything" is a new citizenship and its accompanying new allegiance.

Paul says that "our citizenship is in heaven" (Philippians 3:20). We abide in the kingdom while the kingdom is distinct from the world. As kingdom citizens, we live and speak as if Jesus is our ruler, the gospel is our law, the church is our community, and the kingdom's permanence outweighs the temporary concerns of the world. But it's not just citizenship that changes when we're born again—our allegiance changes, too.

The allegiance of those born again belongs to Jesus. But through Jesus, that allegiance extends also to our neighbor. This is the point of parables like the Good Samaritan and directives like the Great Commandment. Jesus makes care for others non-negotiable for kingdom living. John put it this way:

"We know that we have passed from death to life because we love our brothers. The one who does not love remains in death" (1 John 3:14).

The litmus test for whether one has been born again is love for others. This principle was set up by Jesus Himself in John 13:35, when He said:

"By this all people will know that you are My disciples, if you have love for one another."

> **Why do you think love for others is the mark of authentic discipleship?**

When Paul wrote to the church at Philippi, the city was part of a Roman colony. This meant that it was ruled by Roman law rather than native custom and that its citizens were Roman citizens. Many of them were proud of this privilege. Paul turned this civic pride on its head, encouraging them to see themselves belonging to a greater citizenship than that of Rome.

Do we treat it as such? What are some other things we implicitly consider to be the hallmark of truly following Jesus?

The connection between love for God and love for others is inextricable. They cannot be dissected. According to the Bible, it doesn't even make sense to say we love God but don't love others. Peter learned in John 21 that to love Jesus is to feed the sheep. To love God truly is to love others. Jesus solidified this truth in the Great Commandment:

"Love the Lord your God with all your heart, with all your soul, with all your strength, and with all your mind; and your neighbor as yourself" (Luke 10:27).

There is a gospel reason for this connection, which we will explore more fully in the next session on the rhythm of community. But for now it's enough to say that in the mind of Christ, there is not just duplicity in love for God and neglect of neighbor—there is death in it. In fact, this startling reality will come crashing home for many in the end of days:

"Then He will also say to those on the left, 'Depart from Me, you who are cursed, into the eternal fire prepared for the Devil and his angels!

"'For I was hungry and you gave Me nothing to eat; I was thirsty and you gave Me nothing to drink; I was a stranger and you didn't take Me in; I was naked and you didn't clothe Me, sick and in prison and you didn't take care of Me.'

"Then they too will answer, 'Lord, when did we see You hungry, or thirsty, or a stranger, or without clothes, or sick, or in prison, and not help You?'

"Then He will answer them, 'I assure you: Whatever you did not do for one of the least of these, you did not do for Me either'" (Matthew 25:41-45).

It's not just nameless, faceless, needy people we ignore every day— it's Jesus. It's Him we are neglecting, scorning, and shaming. It's Jesus we pass by every day while we're on our track, gazing downward, preoccupied with ourselves and our interests.

"We conclude, therefore, that a Christian lives not in himself, but in Christ and in his neighbor. Otherwise he is not a Christian."
—Martin Luther[59]

Author and speaker Jen Hatmaker deals with this passage of Scripture at length in her Threads study, *Interrupted*. At *threadsmedia. com/interrupted*, you can read more about Jen and download a sample session from her study.

In a very real spiritual sense, then, to abide in Christ means to abide in our neighbors. Certainly in a physical sense, to abide in Christ means to abide in the presence of our neighbors, caring for and comforting them, loving them at the very least as much as we love ourselves. When we treat our faith consumeristically, we keep Jesus, and consequently others, at a distance. But when we get closer to Jesus, we get closer to others, drawn both to Him and to those He leads us to.

The good news is that being born again empowers and equips us to love others; the rhythms of the kingdom include this rhythm of service and generosity, and this rhythm is something God produces in and through us.

In what ways does abiding in Christ influence abiding in the presence of your neighbors?

Why would God care how you treat others? Why doesn't He just ask you to "live and let live," leaving everybody alone?

What other verses or passages of Scripture can you think of that in some way connect allegiance to God with love for others?

Listen to "Reconciliation," an audio devotion from author Jared C. Wilson. Your group leader can send it to you via e-mail. As you listen, consider the relationship between obedience and reconciliation.

For a challenging look at how the church should be operating in the world, read *Servolution* by Dino Rizzo.

GENEROUS HEARTS

As we've learned, Jesus refocused the spiritual concern on the heart in the Sermon on the Mount. This is why in Matthew 4:21-30 He said that hating is equivalent to murder and lusting is the same as committing adultery. The sin begins not with our outward behaviors but with our inner thoughts. It doesn't come from the external, but from within. That's why in Matthew 15:11 Jesus said it's not what goes into us that makes us unclean, but what comes out. He wants us to know that the heart is the seat of our true character.

This principle has great implications for service and generosity. Jesus articulated it this way in the Sermon:

"But when you give to the poor, don't let your left hand know what your right hand is doing, so that your giving may be in secret. And your Father who sees in secret will reward you" (Matthew 6:3-4).

This passage references the same pride prohibited in Jesus' words on fasting earlier in the Sermon. Giving in secret also has another layer of meaning here. Its true meaning runs deeper than just not making a show of one's giving. Giving in secret can refer to the seat of our giving, the secret place inside of us—our heart. Giving in secret in this case means to give from a place of heartfelt generosity.

Why make this distinction? Because if we focus on the "doing" of serving apart from the "being" of generosity, we are at once engaged in works-righteousness. You can be as self-righteous as the showiest Pharisee without anyone knowing it. Or if you're giving for self-satisfaction, to earn points with God, or to impress the recipient of your gift, you are giving in secret but doing so from a stingy heart.

Generosity should always begin with the heart. Paul wrote:

"Each person should do as he has decided in his heart—not out of regret or out of necessity, for God loves a cheerful giver" (2 Corinthians 9:7).

When we find the rhythm of service from within the counter-cultural kingdom of God, it cultivates in our hearts an increase in generosity. Just as exercise strengthens our hearts over time by stressing them in times of controlled exertion, we strengthen our hearts in the blessing of generosity as we practice being generous with others.

> What does Paul mean by "a cheerful giver" in 2 Corinthians 9:7?

> List some modern examples of "doing" generosity without really "being" generous.

> Describe your own level of generosity and service. Do you give sacrificially? Do you serve or volunteer in some way?

"Remember this: the person who sows sparingly will also reap sparingly, and the person who sows generously will also reap generously" (2 Corinthians 9:6).

"It's hard to convince the world that Jesus cares when we don't."
— Will and Lisa Samson,
Justice in the Burbs[60]

RECONCILABLE DIFFERENCES

When Jesus wrapped up the Sermon on the Mount at the end of Matthew 7, the very first thing He did was heal a leper. And then He healed a centurion's servant. Then He healed Peter's mother-in-law. Then He delivered "many who were demon-possessed" and "healed all who were sick" (Matthew 8:16). Matthew wrote in 8:17 that Jesus did this to fulfill Isaiah's prophecy:

"He Himself took our weaknesses and carried our diseases."

It's no coincidence that all of this amazing stuff happened immediately after the delivery of the Sermon on the Mount. Jesus proclaimed the blueprint for the kingdom of God present on earth. Then He immediately enacted it. In the kingdom, those who mourn are comforted, so Jesus healed people. In the kingdom, those who hunger and thirst for righteousness will be satisfied, so Jesus freed people from demonic oppression. The miracles of healing, deliverance, and provision were signs of kingdom arrival. The miracles of walking on water, multiplying fish and loaves, and healing a blind man with dirt and spit were all signs of the dawning new creation. The miracles were Jesus declaring to us, "I am making everything new!" (Revelation 21:5).

If we mean to walk to the rhythms of the kingdom, we must also show the signs of new creation—renewal, redemption, and the existence of a kingdom unlike the oppressive and destructive kingdoms of the world. Practicing the rhythms of the kingdom simply means acting like the kingdom is real and present—and *meaning it.*

Every time we bind those who are broken, feed those who are hungry, clothe those who are naked, and heal those who are sick, we are living according to the reality of the kingdom.

The apostle Paul reminded us of Jesus' commissioning of His followers to go into all the world and make disciples of all nations by challenging us with a commission of his own.

Read 2 Corinthians 5:14-20. How does Christ's love compel us not to live for ourselves?

In what ways is forgiveness emphasized in this passage?

The commission Paul gave us, in keeping with Christ's commission, is to be ambassadors of the kingdom. Ambassadors are officials who are citizens of one nation but live in another as representatives of the nation of their citizenship. Their job, ideally, is to create goodwill between the nation of their residency and the nation of their citizenship. In most countries, ambassadors are exempt from many of the laws of the nation of their residency, and instead liable to the laws of their citizenship nation. But good ambassadors do not exploit this liberty.

As ambassadors for Christ, Christians run a parallel risk. Because we are under the new covenant of the gospel and our allegiance is to Christ, we have diplomatic immunity from the curse of the law, sin, and death. Nevertheless, like good ambassadors we seek the glory of our citizenship nation in our service to the nation of our residency. We realize that the best representation of our true kingdom is a life of generosity to and sacrifice for those outside the kingdom.

But unlike "real world" diplomacy, the point of kingdom ambassadorship is, as Paul says, pleading on Christ's behalf for reconciliation. Paul even calls the work of Christians "the ministry of reconciliation" (2 Corinthians 5:18). This is the work of Christ in His redemption of new creation. It is the great, glowing picture of the Sermon on the Mount—kingdom restoration in the relational reconciliation between God and man, and then between men as a result.

How does generosity in the kingdom of your residency bring glory to the kingdom of your citizenship?

What does that look like in your everyday life?

Every two years, the city of Corinth hosted an athletic contest called the Isthmian Games. Great numbers of tourists would travel to the city, creating a natural intersection of cultures. Because of their familiarity with the rest of the world, Paul's "ambassador" language would have been very meaningful to his audience.

"The kingdom of God flows through those who are open to being dispensers of God's love and presence."
— Steve Sjogren[61]

Listen to "By Our Love" by Christy Nockels from the *Abide* playlist. Your group leader can e-mail you the entire list, or you can find it at *threadsmedia.com/abide*.

SERVANTHOOD

There's no getting around it: service is servanthood. While the spirit of our age appeals to our desire to master ourselves and others, the kingdom calls for humility and self-denial. The kingdom calls for decrease.

The messiah-king everyone expected in Jesus' day was a revolutionary hero, a military warrior who would violently overthrow the kingdoms of the world in order to establish the kingdom of God. Instead they got a foot-washing carpenter. When the world was looking for a zealot, they got a servant instead. Jesus declared the success of this reversal in Matthew 5:5 when He said, "Blessed are the gentle, because they will inherit the earth."

Soon thereafter, Jesus began talking about going a second mile with someone who demands the first, giving to anyone who makes requests, and—scariest of all—loving our enemies. In all of this we see the upside-down nature of kingdom subversion. The kingdoms of the world trade in rhythms like accumulation, force, appearance, and individualism. But the kingdom of God exhibits rhythms that rely on God's power rather than ours. They emerge from and point to the greatness of God, not the greatness of ourselves.

To enlist in the kingdom you must humble yourself; to war for the kingdom you must give of yourself and serve. Mark 10:45 tells us:

"For even the Son of Man did not come to be served, but to serve, and to give His life—a ransom for many."

The problem is that we are constantly using—rather than serving—others. We practice relational legalism, expecting others to serve us, or at least contribute to our own well-being. Our feelings become the measure of a person's worth, and we disdain any who don't measure up. We say implicitly (or explicitly, for that matter) to others that we will serve them after they've earned it somehow.

But nowhere in the Sermon on the Mount did Jesus make the work of the kingdom conditional on the recipient of blessings. He never once violated the spirit of 1 Corinthians 13, a passage that separates love from both feelings and reciprocity. He simply said, "The kingdom is here and this is how it impacts all these different people . . ."

The Beatitudes are actually a great standard for practicing the rhythm of joyful service. They show us what to aim for in our ministry of reconciliation. But more than that, they show us what our service will accomplish. If we will live according to the kingdom, the Beatitudes will come true.

Take a look at the Beatitudes once again in Matthew 5:1-11. What are some practical ways you could minister the blessings described there so others would be blessed?

"Missions is the automatic outflow and overflow of love for Christ. We delight to enlarge our joy in Him by extending it to others."
—John Piper[62]

Now take a look at Matthew 20:20-28:

"Then the mother of Zebedee's sons approached Him with her sons. She knelt down to ask Him for something. 'What do you want?' He asked her.

"'Promise,' she said to Him, 'that these two sons of mine may sit, one on Your right and the other on Your left, in Your kingdom.'

"But Jesus answered, 'You don't know what you're asking. Are you able to drink the cup that I am about to drink?'

"'We are able,' they said to Him. He told them, 'You will indeed drink My cup. But to sit at My right and left is not Mine to give; instead, it belongs to those for whom it has been prepared by My Father.'

"When the 10 disciples heard this, they became indignant with the two brothers. But Jesus called them over and said, 'You know that the rulers of the Gentiles dominate them, and the men of high position exercise power over them. It must not be like that among you. On the contrary, whoever wants to become great among you must be your servant, and whoever wants to be first among you must be your slave; just as the Son of Man did not come to be served, but to serve, and to give His life—a ransom for many.'"

What aspect of this exchange represents the concerns of a consumerist culture?

What is the difference Jesus mentions between the world of the Gentile kingdom and God's kingdom?

Why does Jesus prescribe servanthood and slavery? What's the significance of these traits?

How might your answers to the previous question relate to the work of local and world missions?

THE BLESSED EMPTINESS

The formula is simple: We are only able to love because God first loved us. First John 4:19 says so.

The formula for service runs parallel: Jesus gave His life as a ransom for many, so we are to give our lives to others as well. The rhythm of service is so much greater than merely handing change to a beggar or dropping off a donation at Goodwill. The word *rhythm* itself implies regularity, sustainability, and continuation. The life of servanthood is supposed to be just that—a life. That is, after all, what Jesus gave to us.

The rhythm of service calls for a heart beating with generosity, a posture of sacrifice, and a vision of compassion in the world. It means repenting of relational legalism, the exploitation of the weak, the ignoring of our neighbor, and the neglect of others. It means repenting of not noticing.

Paul found the joy in this humble servitude, this sacrificial service:

"But even if I am poured out as a drink offering on the sacrifice and service of your faith, I am glad and rejoice with all of you" (Philippians 2:17).

The image of being poured out is powerful. It reflects emptying. It establishes the poured-out life of Christ at the cross as the central motivation for service to others. We are constantly filling ourselves up with all sorts of things that are typically not very good for us.

If you're following the trajectory of this study closely, you noticed that the first two sessions dealt with rhythms that provide sustenance to the Christian life: Bible study and prayer. When we are full from these provisions, we can then make room in our lives by fasting. And when we have the resources of Scripture and intimacy with God along with the freedom of fasting, we are then able to give and serve with joy. These are all the rhythms Jesus practiced in order to present Himself a worthy sacrifice for the debt of sin.

Lift up your eyes and see that Jesus has stooped down low to us.

Earlier in Philippians 2, Paul set up the gospel of Christ's self-emptying and humility:

"Make your own attitude that of Christ Jesus, who, existing in the form of God, did not consider equality with God as something to be used for His own advantage. Instead He emptied Himself by assuming the form of a slave, taking on the likeness of men. And when He had come as a man in His external form, He humbled Himself by becoming obedient to the point of death—even to death on a cross. For this reason God also highly exalted Him and gave Him the name that is above every name, so that at the name of Jesus every knee should bow—of those who are in heaven and on earth and under the earth—and every tongue should confess that Jesus Christ is Lord, to the glory of God the Father" (Philippians 2:5-11).

This beautiful proclamation of the blessed emptiness of Jesus Christ makes our service possible and powerful. What an amazing God we have that He takes the route of subservience and sacrificial death to best establish the sovereignty and supremacy of His Son!

This can only mean that our service and sacrifice are what will demonstrate that Christ—not we—is sovereign over our lives and that Christ—not we—is supreme in our lives.

"I was made a servant of this gospel by the gift of God's grace that was given to me by the working of His power" (Ephesians 3:7).

Many scholars believe this portion of Philippians 2 is a hymn that was sung by the early church.

A CLOSING PRAYER

"Remember, Lord, all the infants, the children, the youth, the young, the middle-aged, and the elderly who are hungry, sick, thirsty, naked, captive, or friendless in this world. Be with those who are tempted with suicide, sick in soul, those who are in despair.

"Remember those who are in prison, all those who are under sentence of death. Remember the widows and widowers, the orphans, and those who travel in a foreign land. Remember all who this day will work under oppressive conditions. Remember the lonely."

—Taken from *Devotional Classics*[63]

GET RHYTHM

This week, notice your own rhythms. Spend 60 seconds listening to yourself breathe. What do you notice about the way it sounds? What sensations do you have as you breathe? What other rhythms are a part of your life? Use the space in the following pages to journal what you hear and think about.

RHYTHM PRACTICE

Comb through a few pages of the day's newspaper and begin making a list of people to pray for based on the news stories (or even the obituaries). Then turn your prayer time during the week into a time of focused prayer for the strangers you now know are in need. Use the space in the following pages to journal about your experience.

RHYTHM FIVE
GENUINE COMMUNITY

Suburbia likes to think it's good at community. From the PTO to public parks, we play at the illusion of community.

The most visible example of this illusion is the coffee shop. Coffee shops are often set up to look like a living room. Starbucks, for instance, provides couches, love seats, and even board games. Most coffee shops are trying to become the leading "third place" in American culture, the place people gather besides work or home. People come to third places, apart from obligation, in order to experience community.

But what the coffee shops (and the cafes, and probably even the bars these days) actually provide is a place for neighbors to come be alone together. When I'm in a coffee shop, I'm usually by myself to work or relax, surrounded by other lonesome souls with headphones in their ears and laptops in their faces. We all do our best not to bother each other.

The architecture and infrastructure of suburbia itself also reflects the shift in our culture from actual community to the illusion of community. Most suburban homes are built very close together in neighborhoods with a high density of houses. That proximity would suggest that we want to be involved in each other's lives. But if we look more closely, we see that nothing could be further from the truth.

Once upon a time, the front porch was the place to be. You sat outside and greeted those who passed. You knew your neighbors—or at least knew their names—and community life was the fabric of social success. But today's suburban homes are pushed way back from the street. And the "sitting out" activity has moved from the front porch to the back deck. Even the design of the homes themselves has changed, with the most livable rooms pushed to the rear of houses, separated by foyers and hallways and dens we rarely use. We now live in the day of privacy fences rather than front porches. Reflecting on this situation, author Skye Jethani surmises, "Everything about suburban home design communicates to the passerby, 'Leave me alone!'"[64]

THE CUSTOMER-DRIVEN CHURCH

All of this environmental insulation, lived so ironically in close proximity to others, creates a dysfunction in us about the idea of community and the gospel of reconciliation. And it has severe ramifications for church life.

The life of Christian discipleship is designed to be lived in community. The old covenant was made with God's chosen people, and the new covenant is made with God's called-out people. Jesus began His ministry with 12 friends and assorted other hangers-on. The Book of Acts details the birth of the church as it did life together. The rest of the New Testament is written to church communities.

As Paul wrote, one part of a body can't say to another, "I don't need you!" (1 Corinthians 12:21).

But we live both our spiritual and physical lives behind a big "Do Not Disturb" sign. Jesus ignores such signs. He doesn't care one iota about your personal space. He knows, and we should admit, that we desperately need to be disturbed.

> **Do you think our culture values privacy or community? How can you tell?**

> **If it's true that we only want the illusion of community, how differently would authentic community look from what we have?**

The very presence of the church in suburban neighborhoods should be a constant, living proclamation—a lighthouse of the benefits and blessings of community. Especially today, this *must* mean embodying the biblically-prescribed counter-culture of the kingdom, challenging everyone who lives in the world to not live as those who are *of* it. But instead of living the subversive message of Jesus, suburban churches often reflect and emulate their cultures rather than challenge them. We've opted for being a mirror rather than a light.

To be the light will take a pretty radical adjustment in perspective for most churches. Suburban churches will have to start thinking of

"I pray not only for these, but also for those who believe in Me through their message. May they all be one, as You, Father, are in Me and I am in You. May they also be one in Us, so the world may believe You sent me. I have given them the glory You have given Me. May they be one as We are one" (John 17:20-22).

"In our experience, people are often enthusiastic about community until it impinges on their decision-making."
—Tim Chester and Steve Timmis, *Total Church*[65]

their ministries less as places where religious goods and services are provided and more as training centers where the community is inspired and empowered by the regular preaching of the gospel. In such a training center, people are learning as they go how to follow Jesus and serve each other in His name.

Because we're all consumers at heart, the business of a local church as a provider of spiritual goods and services to Christian consumers is pervasive and difficult to counteract. Our culture both feeds our consumption and stirs up desires for more and more within us. A church that appeals to our passivity and reflects our susceptibility to shiny things, appetites, and pride is many times the most appealing option. A church that requires only a little bit of commitment, but primarily supplies a vast array of programs, classes, and services will do extremely well in our consumer culture.

In fact, many of us choose church communities not because of brotherhood, relational connection, or submission to the idea of community itself, but because the music is better than the music of other churches. Or because the services are at more convenient times. Or because the youth ministry is well resourced.

What about you? Why did you choose the current church you're a part of?

Are the programs in most churches wrong? When do they become wrong?

The result of all this is the customer-driven church, where everything is tailored and marketed directly for maximum impact among maximum crowds. There are two problems: First of all, the entry point for the kingdom is the denial and crucifixion of self. In the customer-driven church, the churchgoer is in the seat of honor. The customer, as they say, is always right.

And that leads to the second problem: every church hosts multiple customers. When we're all there for ourselves, not only do we fail to

The Radical Reformission by Mark Driscoll is a book designed to help Christians rethink the purpose of the church. It will challenge you to start thinking of the church in terms of what it can give, rather than what you can get.

"The value of family and con-gregational unity is drowned out by consumerism's mantra of individual choice. Customiza-tion has replaced community as a core value of worship."
—Skye Jethani[66]

"If anyone wants to come with Me, he must deny himself, take up his cross daily, and follow Me" (Luke 9:23).

reap the best benefits of Christian discipleship, but we're barely even a church. There is no concept of the church in the New Testament as a collection of individuals with individual ambitions and preferences. Instead, we find a single-minded group driven from the outside by the Spirit of God and mechanized on the inside by the unity of community.

That's not to say churches aren't trying. But the dirty little secret of modern church programming is that small group programs aren't working very well. We all recognize they're key to cultivating the need for community in our churches, but most of us also recognize they're notoriously difficult to pull off. There are a lot of reasons for this, but primarily they all boil down to the fact that American Christians don't want to experience community. Or, at least, they want other things *more*.

At the outset of creation, God looked at solitary Adam and announced that it's not good for man to be alone. In the day of the customer-driven church, we basically respond, "Nah, it'll be OK."

But we are not OK.

Describe your own experience in church with the concept of community. Has it been easy or difficult?

What has prevented you from engaging in regular Christian community in the past?

Why would God design discipleship to be done in community? Why wouldn't He just create personalized, individual plans?

THE SALVATION COMMUNITY

Amazingly, the gospel doesn't stop at reconciling man and God; it also reconciles man and man. We see the original division between mankind in the fall of Adam and Eve. Part of the curse that came as a

Perhaps the most well-known writing regarding Christian community is *Life Together* by Dietrich Bonhoeffer. This short book deserves a place on your shelf.

result of their disobedience is relational conflict. Ever since Adam and Eve, people have lived in disharmony and isolation from each other. This division was first most vividly illustrated when Cain dismissed the idea that he be Abel's keeper.

Because the division caused by sin is an all-encompassing division—cutting us off from.God and, therefore, from each other—the gospel is an all-encompassing remedy. Jesus' atoning work reconciles us to God, but it also reconciles us to each other. Or, rather, it should. The gospel creates the culture of reconciliation, which the New Testament calls the church.

Peter elaborated on the nature of the church this way:

"But you are a chosen race, a royal priesthood, a holy nation, a people for His possession, so that you may proclaim the praises of the One who called you out of darkness into His marvelous light. Once you were not a people, but now you are God's people" (1 Peter 2:9-10a).

> **What do all of Peter's descriptors for the church have in common?**

> **What is the meaning of "Once you were not a people, but now you are God's people"?**

> **According to this passage, what is the purpose of the church?**

Many of us are familiar with the powerful picture of Christian community and the ideal portrait of church ministry recorded in Acts 2. Luke's description of the church's activity in this passage has become the goal of many churches that desire to cultivate community. But two chapters later, Luke reiterated the miraculous ministry of the church in a more expansive and illustrative way.

Paul dealt at length with how the gospel brings people together in the Book of Ephesians. Particularly in chapter 2, he described the "dividing wall of hostility"(2:14) between Jews and Gentiles. He may have been thinking of the literal wall in the temple that separated the two ethnic groups. In Christ, however, that wall is demolished.

"Christian brotherhood is not an ideal which we must realize; it is rather a reality created by God in Christ in which we may participate." —Dietrich Bonhoeffer[68]

Please read Acts 4:23-35 carefully. What stands out most to you?

This passage records what happened just after Peter and John were released from Sanhedrin custody. It's worth noting that Peter and John returned to their church family and reported that the Sanhedrin had warned them not to continue preaching the gospel. Indeed if they kept on preaching, it would cost them greatly, perhaps even their lives. The response of the church was amazing. Instead of falling into a spirit of despair, they responded in praise and prayer. Their prayer was so stirring, the building shook with the presence of the Spirit.

According to this passage, what were the qualities of the Acts 4 church?

Find your favorite online Bible search engine and search for the phrases "one another" and "each other." The results are eye-opening.

Where do you see the four previously covered kingdom rhythms—Scripture, prayer, fasting, and service—in this passage?

What we see in Acts 4 is the full concert of the rhythms of the kingdom in their proper context—the Christian community. The Acts 4 church felt Scripture together, prayed together, fasted together, and served one another together. Today's church should do no less.

As independent consumers, we might easily make the mistake of using a book like *Abide* for our personal journey. But none of the kingdom rhythms can be sustained independently. While the gospel announces salvation for individuals, it also brings about a community of salvation. We need each other. The Christian life must be walked within the encouragement, edification, and accountability of Christian community. We need teachers to teach us how to do it, encouragers to inspire and sustain us, givers to remind us to give, helpers to help us embrace servitude, and prophets to speak truth to us.

The New Testament uses a couple of words that are translated "church." The Greek *kyriakon* means "thing belonging to the Lord." *Ekklesia* refers to an "assembly."

To abide in Christ necessitates embracing the body of Christ as God's plan for living the Christian life. Abiding in Christ can't be fully experienced apart from abiding in the community that bears Jesus' name. Even further, embracing kingdom rhythms becomes easier and more sustainable when it's done alongside others.

FEELING SCRIPTURE IN COMMUNITY

Many of us have learned how rewarding studying the Bible with other believers can be. Studying Scripture with others will take you places in the Bible you might not venture on your own. This, too, enhances your ability to feel Scripture.

God has gifted some Christians to be teachers, but even if you happen to be one of those people, you still need to experience the teaching of others. What we see in the snapshots of the early church in the New Testament is the called-out community devoting themselves to the teaching of the apostles. That's plural—the apostles together. In Acts 4, they prayed "unanimously" words from the Old Testament. In other depictions they learned together and discussed. In still others they gathered and listened to preaching. There is an "iron sharpening iron" principle at work in these gatherings.

In Ephesians 4, Paul described various people in the church. He claimed that some people are gifted to be teachers, others prophets, others pastors. But the goal of those leaders is the "training of the saints in the work of ministry" (v. 12).

From the large gathering of a worship service to the more intimate small groups, Bible study in the early church was a team event. Perhaps the best way to cultivate a feeling for Scripture is by experiencing bold preaching and devoted community groups. As you study Scripture together, you begin to interpret it through a communal lens, pondering its implications not just for your individual life but for your church.

What are some other benefits of studying Scripture in group settings?

Listen to "Intentionality," an audio devotion from author Jared C. Wilson. Your group leader can send it to you via e-mail. As you listen, think about how far out of your way you are willing to go for relationships.

What might be some pitfalls of group Bible study?

How can group study help individuals develop a feel for Scripture?

PRAYER IN COMMUNITY

We learn to pray by praying together. There is no more intimate moment with our brothers and sisters in Christ than collectively approaching the throne room of God through Christ and in the Spirit. In communal prayer, we reveal the desires and depressions of our hearts. We share our burdens. We connect to each other as we connect to God.

One of the key ways relational intimacy develops in times of shared prayer is through confession. The first thing we ought to confess is our sin of not confessing our sins to each other. James wrote, "Therefore, confess your sins to one another and pray for one another, so that you may be healed" (5:16a). Is there anything more absent from group prayer than confession? I believe our reluctance and fear to confess sins to each other is a direct result of our failure to cultivate authentic community in our churches.

Confession and community feed each other: Confession creates communal intimacy, and communal intimacy produces confession. But that's not all. When we confess our sins to each other, we set up the opportunity to share the gospel with each other, and there's no greater privilege God gives us than to share the good news.

Just think about it—as we confess our sins to God and others, fellow Christians can step into our prayers and say right back to us the good news of Jesus. When we receive each other's confessions, we can remind each other of the truths we so easily forget in the midst of despair: Jesus loves us; He died to reconcile us to God; there's no condemnation for those who are in Christ.

Another aspect of communal prayer is the celebration of the Lord's Supper. This is actually a required work of the church community. Whether you're eating the Lord's Supper in a small group or in a worship service, the family meal of Christ's body and blood is the most powerful and Christ-exalting way to proclaim the gospel to each other.

> **What are some reasons Christians don't confess their sins to each other?**

> **How might we create more "safety" for honest confession in Christian community?**

The 2002 film *About a Boy* is the story of how a lonely and misunderstood child taught a self-centered and closed man the importance of living in community. Gather your own group of friends to learn why no man is an island.

Listen to "Abide" by Jacob's Well from the *Abide* playlist. Use this playlist as the soundtrack for your study. Your group leader can e-mail it to you, or you can find it at *threadsmedia.com/abide*.

Why wouldn't eating the Lord's Supper by yourself be ideal?

The original celebration of the Lord's Supper was much different than what we experience today. Called "The Love Feast," it was a full meal and had the feeling of a celebration.

FASTING IN COMMUNITY

Perhaps the biggest failure of contemporary Christian community is the failure to fast. A wise man once said, "Show me your budget, and I'll show you your god." Unfortunately even the church itself might have some explaining to do in this regard. If the Great Commandment is to love our neighbors as ourselves, and if the body of Christ is to do what Christ did, which was lay His life down as a ransom for many, how should this be reflected in what we indulge in financially or with other resources? How should it be reflected in what we *don't* indulge in?

Do our churches reflect a communal effort to joyfully fast from the accessories and amenities of consumer-driven church? These days fewer and fewer people give financially to their church, and fewer and fewer churches give financially to missions.[69]

A *Christianity Today* feature article tells the story of Francis Chan, pastor of Cornerstone Church in Simi Valley, California, and their radical efforts to fast with purpose:

> "When Cornerstone started, growth had been the goal—get bigger and better. But in 1999, a missionary from Papua New Guinea pointed out that Cornerstone's whole focus seemed to be on themselves. Chan now admits, 'I was very self-centered, and therefore, I led a church into being self-centered.'

> "In 2002, a trip to Uganda changed Chan forever. There he saw real poverty, and it became personal. Little girls the age of his daughters rooted through dumpsters for food. Chan began to ask himself, *What does it look like to love my neighbor as myself?*

> "His answer was to move his family of four out of their 2,000-square-foot house into one half that size so they could give more to missions. 'I couldn't reconcile how I could live in such a nice house while others were starving,' Chan says . . .

> "Convicted by the verse to 'love your neighbor as yourself,' Chan showed up at the next board meeting with an agenda. In the early years, Cornerstone gave away four percent of its budget.

Crazy Love by Francis Chan is a compelling read that reinforces how God's love for us in the gospel is meant to overflow into our love for others.

Chan asked them to give away 50 percent. Cuts in staff salaries and serious sacrifices in programs would have to be made, but it only took a half hour for the board to agree . . .

"In 2008 the church will give away 55 percent of its budget to the poor and hungry through various ministries, including a $1 million annual commitment to Children's Hunger Fund and a sizeable contribution to World Impact, which plants churches in urban America."[70]

That is a church dedicated to purposeful fasting! They are foregoing what they could easily afford in order to care for others. The example of Chan and Cornerstone continues to influence other churches as well.

In 2008, the church plant I pastored was inspired by Cornerstone's stunning self-emptying, and our leadership decided to commit 60 percent of our budget to local and foreign missions. Sustaining the church's operations on 40 percent of offerings wasn't easy, but none of our community regretted the restraint of meager resources. We fasted joyfully.

Why do you think many churches find it difficult to send as much money out the door as they keep inside?

What would happen in your church if the mission budget was raised to 50 percent of the entire church budget?

What does a church's fasting look like in its community? Does it involve more than just money? What would it communicate to people outside the church?

SERVICE IN COMMUNITY
Dietrich Bonhoeffer called the church "the new humanity of Christ."[72] This means that the church isn't called the body of Christ for theoretical

Giving by North American churchgoers was higher during the Great Depression (3.3 percent of per capita income in 1933) than it was after a half-century of unprecedented prosperity (2.5 percent in 2004).[71]

Bonhoeffer's idea is linked firmly to Paul's writings. In Ephesians, Paul wrote about the one new man who is formed in Christ. The new man is the church.

reasons. Instead, the church is charged with carrying on the continuing mission of Jesus in the world. Literally. We are meant to do what the physical body of Christ did—preach and teach, comfort and care, heal and restore, build and create, feed and fix.

Jesus called His disciples to Him, and His disciples followed Him as He ministered the gospel of the kingdom near and far. It makes little biblical sense for the church today to function as if its central mission is facilitating personal spirituality through the "grocery store" style discipleship of church programs. In this manner, members can pick and choose what they participate in according to their taste. Our sense of mission—which is the *modus operandi* of the New Testament church—is skewed, if not quenched.

Thankfully, many churches in the Western world are beginning to regain a sense of God's call to love their neighbors in service and generosity. When we take the love of Christ into our communities, cities, nations, and eventually the ends of the earth, we are truly fulfilling the call to the church to be the hands and feet of Jesus.

In what ways are you personally serving others outside the church?

In what ways is your church community serving others outside the church?

If Jesus' ministry and mission looked like the ministry and mission being conducted by the modern church, what would He be doing?

CITY ON A HILL

The brilliant, God-designed blueprint for kingdom life in Jesus' Sermon on the Mount envisions a community called, formed, and led by God into worship and outward mission that invites a lost world to behold the glory of God. When we, as a community of Christ-followers, demonstrate our collective life in Christ through feeling Scripture,

At your meeting time this week, watch the video called "Fences." As you do, consider how committed you are to privacy. What are the fences in your own life?

Ninety percent of the 4.4 billion people living in the so-called "10/40 window"—the area of the world that lies across Africa and Asia from 10 degrees latitude north of the equator to 40 degrees latitude north of the equator—are unevangelized.[73]

intentional prayer, purposeful fasting, radical generosity, and relational intimacy, we create a compelling announcement of the kingdom's presence in the world. This compelling announcement is what Jesus referred to in the Sermon in Matthew 5:13-16:

"You are the salt of the earth. But if the salt should lose its taste, how can it be made salty? It's no longer good for anything but to be thrown out and trampled on by men.

"You are the light of the world. A city situated on a hill cannot be hidden. No one lights a lamp and puts it under a basket, but rather on a lampstand, and it gives light for all who are in the house. In the same way, let your light shine before men, so that they may see your good works and give glory to your Father in heaven."

When we read Jesus' words about being the salt of the earth, we often think He was talking about preservation. That's what salt was used for—to preserve food. So when we are "salty," we preserve the message of the gospel. While there is an element of truth in that, Jesus' metaphor goes further. In His day, phrases like "salty speech" referred to "flavor." So Jesus was referencing the church adding "spice" to life— being compelling in its message and mission.

Paul appealed to the same notion in Colossians 4:6:

"Your speech should always be gracious, seasoned with salt, so that you may know how you should answer each person."

The church gives the compelling appeal of salt in the earth by making the good news sound and look good.

How can a church make the good news sound good?

Do you think we as the church struggle to make the good news look good? Why?

If you're in the mood for a heavy read, launch into *City of God*, written in the Fifth century by Augustine of Hippo. In it, he discusses politics, philosophy, and other matters through the lens of gospel living.

"We need Christian communities who saturate ordinary life with the gospel."
—Tim Chester and Steve Timmis[74]

The other image Jesus offered in this passage is of a city on a hill, a shining tower of hope set apart but illuminating for all those around. This image doesn't mean the church is to be distant in proximity from the world, but rather that the church should be visible to the world in the same way as a shining light in the darkness. The problem today is that many churches are very noticeable and flashy, but their light shines on themselves. They broadcast their own greatness. But Jesus' aim in the Sermon on the Mount is the glory of God.

When we get right down to it, it's the difference between being a consumer-driven church and being a missional church. In an ideal world, the idea of a "missional church" would be redundant, because the church by definition is supposed to be missional.

The two great failures of the evangelical church today are failures of the highest magnitude: neglected proclamation of the gospel and refused embodiment of the gospel.

In 1 Corinthians 15:3-4 Paul defined the gospel as "most important." There is nothing more important than the good news that Jesus Christ died for sinners and rose again. This gospel is the primary message of the kingdom and the primary catalyst of the kingdom's spread. The gospel is power. And yet consumer Christianity has essentially relegated it to the backseat of message and mission.

We ought to take great care that we don't unintentionally perpetuate the errors of preaching a gospel we don't embody or embodying a gospel we don't preach. Neither error is truly gospel. Both are attempts at talking about a rhythm without charting or playing it.

We must embrace both gospel-driven proclamation and gospel-driven servanthood, for both are vital to the ministry of reconciliation. Our world is at war. There is no square inch of this world that isn't claimed by God and counter-claimed by Satan.

Jesus is King, now and forever. The work of the kingdom will lay waste to the gates of hell, but if you are neither speaking Jesus nor being Jesus, you will be part of the rubble left behind.

The call to salt and light is a call to a two-fisted gospel. It's a call to crucify the idols of self and comfort and convenience and relevance, and to give ourselves away. The two-fisted gospel uses one fist to take out the prince of the air with the revolutionary news that the risen Christ is Lord, and one fist to bring justice to the captives with the

Further explore the importance of missional community in *Sent: Living the Missional Nature of the Church* by Ed Stetzer, available from Threads. Visit *threadsmedia. com/sent* for more information.

"Mission in Acts is measured by the spread of the Word and the community it formed."
— Michael Horton[75]

embodied news that God is love. Think of the brightness such light would have. Think of the flavor such salt would add. A loving force of that magnitude couldn't be stopped; the gates of hell will not prevail against it.

The rhythms of the kingdom, when played by the church community like a great biblical symphony, will sustain a worship song so powerful we will taste heaven and broadcast to others the all-surpassing glory of God.

How could the five kingdom rhythms reflect the church's nature of salt and light?

How does your church compare to the kingdom blueprint of the Sermon on the Mount?

How does practicing the kingdom rhythms in Christian community make abiding in Christ seem more natural?

ABIDE

The rhythms of suburbia call us to make our faith personal, private, individual, insulated, and self-protected. Consequently, our faith is often only as public as the Jesus fish on our bumper.

The rhythms of the kingdom, however, call us to get outside of ourselves—indeed, to nail ourselves to the cross—and embrace living for the glory of God and the good of the world.

The knowledge of God's glory will someday cover the earth like the waters cover the sea (Habakkuk 2:14). What a great opportunity we have to begin turning over the coffee shop tables (including the ones in the church atrium) with humble zeal for the spread of the kingdom.

"So they went out and traveled from village to village, proclaiming the good news and healing everywhere" (Luke 9:6).

The Book of Habakkuk is incredibly interesting, especially when you consider the context. The book is essentially a prayer from the prophet to God, wondering about God's decision to use a pagan people to discipline Israel.

The kingdom-created community known as the church is God's designated instrument for sustainable life in Christ. This is why the clearly and regularly preached and demonstrated gospel is so important—because the gospel reminds us that the work is done and it's time to rest and bask in the accomplishment of Jesus.

Therefore, the Christian life should be one marked by Sabbath. The word "abide" implies that there is a different way to live when Christ is involved. Everybody lives, but only a few "abide"—that word creates the distinct sense of rest even while we go about the daily routine. That rest is a gentle but powerful reminder of the good news that "It is finished!," that Christ has declared "Enough!" to sin and death and the curse of the law. You can't merit God's favor and *you don't have to.*

This is what makes the good news of the gospel great news. And this is what makes practicing the rhythms of the kingdom possible and preferable. Under the compulsion of works without the tether of gospel rest, studying the Bible, praying, fasting, giving, and participating in church community can be wearisome. But because of the finished work of Jesus we live in the glorious wake of gospel Sabbath. Inside that rest, we can't help but feel Scripture, speak to our Father, fast with purpose, give generously, and submit to community. These rhythms become not the means to God's love, but the fruit of it.

The gospel is not "I obey, therefore I am approved," but "I am approved, therefore I obey." In the order of the latter, God's work is primary. "We love because He first loved us" (1 John 4:19). The rhythms of the kingdom, then, aren't created by us any more than the kingdom is. They aren't something we "do." The rhythms emanate from God's sovereign reign; they are real ways of "being" in the new creation that has been bearing fruit since Christ's atoning work.

James 2:17 reminds us that faith without works is dead. So make no mistake—there is work to do. But faith provides the mode of "being" for our "doing." It's not our doing that we trust for salvation or spiritual maturity. The gospel isn't just the entry fee to salvation but the currency for all of life. And the good news to be received by faith alone is that Jesus Christ, the very Word of God, interceded for us by fasting from the world's temptations and giving His very life, thereby reconciling us to God and redeeming us into God's family.

So relax.

If you've enjoyed *Abide*, you can read more from Jared C. Wilson on his blog at *gospeldrivenchurch.com*.

A CLOSING PRAYER

"O lover of the loveless, it is thy will that I should love thee with heart, soul, mind, strength, and my neighbour as myself. But I am not sufficient for these things. There is by nature no pure love in my soul; every affection in me is turned from thee; I am bound, as slave to lust, I cannot love thee, lovely as thou art, until thou dost set me free.

"Spirit of love, make me like the loving Jesus; give me his benevolent temper, his beneficent actions, that I may shine before men to thy glory. The more thou doest in love in me and by me, humble me the more; keep me meek, lowly, and always ready to give thee honour."

—Taken from *The Valley of Vision*[76]

GET RHYTHM

Continue your experiment into rhythm this week by going for a walk. Think about your gait. Your steps. You might even take some friends with you to compare your walking rhythm with theirs. Use the space in the following pages to journal about the things you notice.

RHYTHM PRACTICE

Schedule a team-building exercise trip to a ropes course, indoor rock climbing facility, or paintball range with your *Abide* Bible study group. Use the space in the following pages to journal about your experience.

END NOTES

INTRODUCTION

1. "Urban/Rural and Inside Outside Metropolitan Area – Census 2000," *U. S. Census Bureau* [online], [cited 29 Oct. 2009]. Available from the Internet: *factfinder.census.gov.*

SESSION 1

2. "Fast food for children and adolescents" *UpToDate* [online], [cited 2 Nov. 2009]. Available from the Internet: *uptodate.com.*

3. "Birth of a Refreshing Idea," *The Chronicle of Coca-Cola* [online], [cited 15 Dec. 2009]. Available from the Internet: *thecoca-colacompany.com.*

4. Dallas Willard, *The Divine Conspiracy* (San Francisco: HarperCollins Publishers, 1998), 106.

5. Greg Hawkins and Cally Parkinson, *Follow Me: What's Next For You?* (South Barrington, IL: Willow Creek Resources, 2008), 114.

6. Lorne C. Sanny, "How to Spend the Day in Prayer," *Christianity Today* [online], 1 Jan. 1993 [cited 20 Nov. 2009]. Available from the Internet: *christianitytoday.com.*

7. Charles Spurgeon, *Lectures to My Students* (Grand Rapids, MI: Zondervan, 1979), 79.

8. N. T. Wright, *Paul: In Fresh Perspective* (Minneapolis, MN: First Fortress Press, 2009), 155.

9. *http://twitter.com/JohnPiper/status/5027319857.*

10. C. S. Lewis, *The Weight of Glory* (New York, NY: HarperCollins Publishers, 1980), 26.

11. *Guinness World Records* [online], [cited 20 Nov. 2009]. Available from the Internet: *guinnessworldrecords.com.*

12. Thomas a Kempis, *Imitation of Christ* (Nashville: Thomas Nelson, 1999), 56-57.

SESSION 2

13. Blaise Pascal, as quoted in Gary Thomas, *Seeking the Face of God* (Eugene, OR: Harvest House Publishers, 1999), 102.

14. "Stressed Americans Leave 460 Million Vacation Days Unused," *Marketing Vox* [online], July 2008 [cited 16 Dec. 2009]. Available from the Internet: *marketingvox.com.*

15. John Ortberg, *The Life You've Always Wanted* (Grand Rapids, Michigan: Zondervan, 1997), 82.

16. Martin Luther, as qoted in *The Book of Positive Quotations* by John Cook, Steve Deger, and Leslie Ann Gibson, (Minneapolis, MN: Fairview Press, 2007), 181.

17. Mark Henderson, "Media multitaskers are in danger of brain overload." *Times* [online], August 25, 2009 [cited 15 Nov. 2009]. Available from the Internet: *timesonline.co.uk/.*

18. John Ortberg, "Time Well Wasted." *Leadership Journal* [online], August 17, 2009 [cited 25 Nov. 2009]. Available from the Internet: *christianitytoday.com.*

19. J. C. Ryle, "Prayer," *Bible Bulletin Board* [online], [cited 24 Nov. 2009]. Available from the Internet: *biblebb.com.*

20. Tim Keller, "Prayer and the Gospel," *Redeemer Presbyterian Church* [online], 2007 [cited 20 Nov. 2009]. Available from the Internet: *redeemer.com.*

21. Walter Marshall, *The Gospel Mystery of Sanctification* (New York, NY: Southwick and Pelsup, 1811), 257.

22. John Piper, *This Momentary Marriage* (Wheaton, IL: Crossway Books, 2009), 56.

23. Charles Spurgeon, "The Fatherhood of God," *The Bible Bulletin Board* [online], 12 Sept. 1858 [cited 10 Dec. 2009]. Available from the Internet: *biblebb.com.*

24. J. I. Packer, *Knowing God* (Downers Grove, IL: InterVarsity Press, 1993), 202.

25. D. A. Carson, *The Sermon on the Mount* (Grand Rapids, Michigan: Baker, 1978), 65.

26. Hugh Latimer, "Sermons Preached Before King Edward the Sixth: (1549), Sermon #5," *Project Canturbury* [online], [cited 21 Nov. 2009]. Available from the Internet: *anglicanhistory.org*.

27. Paul Miller, *A Praying Life* (Colorado Springs, CO: NavPress, 2009), 55.

28. David Hansen, *Long Wandering Prayer* (Downer's Grove, IL: InterVarsity Press, 2001), 11.

29. Joni Eareckson Tada, as quoted in *The Contemporaries Meet the Classics on Prayer* by Leonard Allen (Monroe, LA: Howard Books, 2003), 106.

30. Paul Miller, *A Praying Life* (Colorado Springs, CO: NavPress, 2009), 135.

31. Bill Hybels, as quoted in *The Contemporaries Meet the Classics on Prayer* by Leonard Allen (Monroe, LA: Howard Books, 2003), 86.

32. Arthur Bennett, ed. *The Valley of Vision* (Carlisle, PA: The Banner of Truth Trust, 2006), 266.

SESSION 3

33. John Calvin, as quoted in *Isaiah: God Saves Sinners* by Raymond C. Ortlund, (Wheaton, IL: Crossway Books, 2005), 267.

34. "TopTenREVIEWS Reports Worldwide Pornography Market at Least $97 Billion," *All Business* [online] 12 Mar. 2007, [cited 10 Nov. 2009]. Available from the Internet: *allbusiness.com*.

35. Cited in Skye Jethani, *The Divine Commodity* (Grand Rapids, Michigan: Zondervan, 2009), 108.

36. Rodney Clapp, "Why The Devil Takes VISA," *Christianity Today* [online], October 7, 1996 [cited 15 Nov. 2009]. Available from the Internet: *christianitytoday.com*.

37. Cited in Skye Jethani, *The Divine Commodity* (Grand Rapids, Michigan: Zondervan, 2009), 114.

38. "U.S. National Debt Clock," *Ed Hall* [online], [cited 3 Dec. 2009]. Available from the Internet: *brillig.com/debt_clock*.

39. "Jim Eliot Quotes," *Think Exist* [online], [cited 12 Nov. 2009]. Available from the Internet: *thinkexist.com*.

40. Gary Thomas, *Sacred Pathways* (Grand Rapids, MI: Zondervan, 2002), 96.

41. John Berridge, *The Works of Rev. John Berridge* (London: Simpkin, Marshall, and Co., 1938), 380.

42. John Owen, *The Glory of Christ* (Carlisle, Pennsylvania: Banner of Truth, 2000), 81.

43. Dallas Willard, *The Divine Conspiracy* (San Francisco: HarperCollins Publishers, 1998), 199.

44. Mark Buchanan, "Trapped in the Cult of the Next Thing," *Christianity Today* [online] September 6, 1999, [cited 5 Nov. 2009]. Available from the Internet: *ctlibrary.com*.

45. Shaun Groves, "Home Wrecked," *Shaun Groves* [online], February 27, 2008 [cited 11 Nov. 2009]. Available from the Internet: *shaungroves.com/2008/02/home-wrecked/*.

46. Will and Lisa Samson, *Justice in the Burbs* (Grand Rapids, MI: Baker Books, 2007), 42.

47. "Henry Wadsworth Longfellow Quotes," *Think Exist* [online], [cited 12 Nov. 2009]. Available from the Internet: *thinkexist.com*.

48. Thomas a Kempis, *Imitation of Christ* (Nashville: Thomas Nelson, 1999), 80-81.

SESSION 4

49. Robert Putnam, *Bowling Alone* (New York, NY: Simon and Schuster, 2001), 19.

50. Mark Twain, "New York: A Splendid Desert" in *Mark Twain Himself: A Pictorial Biography* (Columbia, Missouri: University of Missouri, 2002), 82-83.

51. Marcus Bowman, "U. S. Commuting Statistics," *Slide Share* [online], July 2008 [cited 1 Nov. 2009]. Commuting statistical analysis presentation. Available from the Internet: *slideshare.net/marcus.bowman. slides/us-commuting-statistical-analysis*.

52. "Economic factors tap the brakes on traffic congestion," *Texas Transportation Institute* [online], 8 July 2009 [cited 15 Dec. 2009]. Available from the Internet: *tti.tamu.edu*.

53. "How many people will watch Superbowl XLIII?" *HubDub* [online], 2009 [cited 18 Dec. 2009]. Available from the Internet: *hubdub.com*.

54. C. S. Lewis, *The Weight of Glory* (New York: HarperCollins, 2001), 46.

55. "Philanthropy Statistics: Volunteering (Individuals)," *National Philanthropic Trust* [online], 2007 [cited 5 Nov. 2009]. Available from the Internet: *nptrust.org/philanthropy/philanthropy_stats.asp*.

56. Charlie Peacock, *New Way to be Human: A Provocative Look at What it Means to Follow Jesus* (Colorado Springs, CO: Waterbrook Press, 2004), 70.

57. Michael Horton, *The Gospel-Driven Life: Being Good News People in a Bad News World* (Grand Rapids, MI: Baker Books, 2009), 114.

58. Dietrich Bonhoeffer, *Life Together* (New York: Harper and Row, 1954), 25.

59. Martin Luther, "Freedom of a Christian," in *Three Treatises* (Minneapolis, MN: Fortress Press, 1970), 309.

60. Will and Lisa Samson, *Justice in the Burbs* (Grand Rapids, MI: Baker Books, 2007), 92.

61. Steve Sjogren, *Conspiracy of Kindness* (Ventura, CA: Regal Books, 2003), 87.

62. John Piper, *The Dangerous Duty of Delight* (Sisters, OR: Multnomah Publishers, 2001), 71.

63. Lancelot Andrews, as quoted in *Devotional Classics*, edited by Richard Foster and James Bryan Smith (New York: Harper Collins Publishers, 1993), 78.

SESSION 5

64. Skye Jethani, *The Divine Commodity* (Grand Rapids, MI: Zondervan, 2009), 143.

65. Tim Chester and Steve Timmis, *Total Church: A Radical Reshaping Around Gospel and Community* (Wheaton, IL: Crossway Books, 2008), 45.

66. Skye Jethani, *The Divine Commodity* (Grand Rapids, MI: Zondervan, 2009), 126-127.

67. Will and Lisa Samson, *Justice in the Burbs* (Grand Rapids, MI: Baker Books, 2007), 58.

68. Dietrich Bonhoeffer, *Life Together* (New York: Harper and Row Publishers, 1954), 30.

69. Ronald E. Keener, "Giving trends point toward consumer oriented members," *Church Executive Magazine* [online], Jul. 2008 [cited 15 Nov. 2009]. Available from the Internet: *churchexecutive.com*.

70. Jennifer Schuchmann, "Francis Chan's Crazy Love," *Christianity Today* [online], 28 Oct. 2009 [cited 1 Nov. 2009]. Available from the Internet: *christianitytoday.com*.

71. "Stats on Generous Giving," *Generous Giving* [online], 2009 [cited 20 Nov. 2009]. Available from the Internet: *generousgiving.org*.

72. Dietrich Bonhoeffer, *The Cost of Discipleship* (Norwich, UK: SCM-Canterbury Press, 2001), 184.

73. "10/40 Window: Do you need to be stirred?" *Southern Nazarene University* [online], [cited 30 Nov. 2009]. Available from the Internet: *snu.edu*.

74. Tim Chester and Steve Timmis, *Total Church: A Radical Reshaping Around Gospel and Community* (Wheaton, IL: Crossway Books, 2008), 65.

75. Michael Horton, *The Gospel-Driven Life: Being Good News People in a Bad News World* (Grand Rapids, MI: Baker Books, 2009), 210.

76. Arthur Bennett, ed. *The Valley of Vision* (Carlisle, PA: The Banner of Truth Trust, 2006), 250.

WHAT IS THREADS?

WE ARE A COMMUNITY OF YOUNG ADULTS—
people who are piecing the Christian life together, one
experience at a time. Threads is driven by four key markers
that are essential to young adults everywhere, and though
it's always dangerous to categorize people, we think these are
helpful in reminding us why we do what we do.

First of all, we are committed to being responsible. That is,
doing the right thing. Though we're trying to grow in our
understanding of what that is, we're glad we already know what
to do when it comes to recycling, loving our neighbor, tithing, or
giving of our time.

Community is also important to us. We believe we all need
people. People we call when the tire's flat and people we call
when we get the promotion. And it's those people—the day-in-
day-out people—that we want to walk through life with.

Then there's connection. A connection with our church, a connection with somebody who's
willing to walk alongside us and give us a little advice here and there. We'd like a connection
that gives us the opportunity to pour our lives out for somebody else—and that whole
walk alongside us thing, we're willing to do that for someone else, too.

And finally there's depth. Kiddie pools are for kids. We're looking to dive in, head first,
to all the hard-to-talk-about topics, the tough questions, and heavy Scriptures. We're
thinking this is a good thing, because we're in process. We're becoming. And who we're
becoming isn't shallow.

Thanks for jumping in. Be sure and check us out online at:

THREADSMEDIA.COM

STOP BY TO JOIN OUR ONLINE COMMUNITY
AND COME BY TO VISIT OFTEN!

SENT
LIVING THE MISSIONAL NATURE OF THE CHURCH
BY ED STETZER

Through a thorough examination of the church's call to move outside its walls, noted cultural commentator and missiologist Ed Stetzer urges Christ-followers to understand their privilege and responsibility to go into the world and take with them the transforming gospel of Jesus Christ.

ED STETZER *has planted churches in three states and trained pastors and church planters on five continents. He holds two masters degrees and two doctorates, and has written dozens of articles and books. Ed has taught at more than 15 seminaries and is the director of Lifeway Research and Lifeway's missiologist in residence. Find him online at edstetzer.com.*

THE TOUGH SAYINGS OF JESUS II
BY MICHAEL KELLEY

Continue your journey through four more difficult sayings of Jesus. Michael Kelley offers volume II of *Tough Sayings* that examines the parable of the unrighteous manager, the cursing of the fig tree, the death of Lazarus, and Jesus' command to be more righteous than the Pharisees.

MICHAEL KELLEY *lives in Nashville, Tennessee, with his wife and three children. In addition to writing, Michael speaks at events, conferences, and churches across the country and is an editor for Threads. He blogs daily at* michaelkelleyministries.com.

RED REVOLUTION
SEEING THE WORLD THROUGH THE LENS OF CHRIST
BY ADAM THOMASON

Red Revolution acknowledges that we all see the world through our own set of lenses formed by our culture, heritage, and upbringing. Those lenses color everything we see, including each other. Thomason challenges us to embrace our cultural differences, and what we have in common, in order to exalt Christ above everything else.

ADAM THOMASON *is one of the associate pastors of The Village Church, Dallas Northway campus, in addition to being the director and vision-caster for Red Revolution. Adam resides in Dallas, Texas, with his wife and daughter. Find out more at* theredrevolution.com.

FOR DETAILS ON ALL OF THREADS' STUDIES, VISIT *THREADSMEDIA.COM.*

GROUP CONTACT INFORMATION

Name _____ Number _____

E-mail _____

Name _____ Number _____

E-mail _____

Name _____ Number _____

E-mail _____

Name _____ Number _____

E-mail _____

Name _____ Number _____

E-mail _____

Name _____ Number _____

E-mail _____

Name _____ Number _____

E-mail _____

Name _____ Number _____

E-mail _____

Name _____ Number _____

E-mail _____